# Constitutional Law in Ireland

# CONSTITUTIONAL LAW IN IRELAND

*By*

## Dr JENNIFER KAVANAGH

CLARUS PRESS

**Published by**
Clarus Press Ltd,
Griffith Campus,
South Circular Road,
Dublin 8.
www.claruspress.ie


**Typeset by**
Gough Typesetting Services,
Dublin


**Printed by**
SprintPrint
Dublin


**ISBN**
978-1-911611-06-6

*For my parents, Marie and Sean*

# FOREWORD

The 80th anniversary of the coming into force of the Constitution came and went on 29th December 2017 without much fuss or fanfare. Yet there is really a good deal to celebrate and acknowledge, even if the document had — and still has — its flaws and imperfections. Most of all, this is a good time to study constitutional law because there are signs that new life is being breathed back into that document. The Constitution had, of course, never died. As Dr Kavanagh's book shows, it always had a vitally important role in gluing the institutions of State together. So successful was it in fact that, rather paradoxically, it was one of those external instruments that re-inforced a sense of nationhood and loyalty to the 26 county State rather than — as Mr de Valera might have hoped — to a 32 county State.

When, however, I speak of "new life", it is, however, of a revival of that sense of excitement which attached to constitutional law in that golden era which lasted roughly from 1965 to 1985 when the Supreme Court led the way in showing that the Constitution should be read as a human rights affirming document which itself could operate as an instrument of change in an otherwise highly controlled and stagnant society. From whence does my new found optimism derive? I suggest that it in the first instance it comes from the people, the politicians and the courts.

First and foremost are the people of Ireland. No one who experienced the two recent referenda could not but have been impressed by the sense of engagement with the democratic process — ranging from the chivalrous and respectful nature of the debates to the home to vote movements. This was mass democracy at its very finest and, in the words of Art 6(2) of the Constitution, a magnificent example of the people "in final appeal" deciding "all questions of national policy".

Second are the politicians. In the aftermath of the most recent referendum the Taoiseach spoke of a modern Constitution for a modern State. There is reason to hope that across the parties further constitutional reform will ultimately realise that goal, so that in a sense, both the Constitution and the State itself will have, to borrow Lincoln's promise at Gettysburg, a "new birth of freedom."

Third, change is a stirring in the courts. Here what might seem like a purely technical change in constitutional doctrine — the advent of the suspended declaration of unconstitutionality — has the potential to transform judicial attitudes and to bring about a situation where the Supreme Court ends up playing a role like the German Constitutional Court. Why is this? I would contend that, contrary to contemporary conventional wisdom, the Constitution was, on the whole, too radical fully to be absorbed into the bloodstream of our legal and political life and the remedies with which it endowed the courts were too often regarded as too powerful safely to be used with any frequency.

To use the terminology of the 19th century English political scientist, Bagehot, the "efficient" part of the Constitution (i.e., the working as distinct from the large decorative parts) has the potential to effect too radical a change in the structure of our legal system. This is why I contend that as they gradually realised this in the subsequent decades some of the judiciary have baulked at what was been asked of them. Rather than invalidate a law by reference, for example, to the equality guarantees in Art 40.1 or the far-reaching provisions of Art 40.3.1° and Art 40.3.2°, many judges were instinctively happier with the traditional common law method: incremental, bit by bit change, driven often by pragmatic, fact specific and result orientated considerations.

These efficient parts of the Constitution are admittedly demanding and require a good deal of original judicial thinking in order to make them work and to ensure that they assume a contemporary relevance. This type of constitutional law requires a quite different mind-set to that of the traditional common law, namely, to judge the existing law by reference to a set of inherently generalised principles, ("due course of law", "inviolability of the dwelling", "defend and vindicate", "protection of the person", "personal rights" etc.), together with the ultimate power to annul that law in the event that it did not measure up to these constitutional standards. And there is clear evidence that the judiciary are uncomfortable — even unhappy — if they are required to give full effect to the wording of the Constitution because they privately understand that the logical corollary of doing just this would bring about too radical a break with the established — and slightly cosy — world of the common law which many consider to be the true bedrock of our legal system. An example here is, perhaps, supplied by the Supreme Court's decision in *Meath County Council v Murray*[1] where it in effect called for caution in the interpretation of Art 40.5 (guaranteeing the inviolability of the dwelling), precisely because of the potentially far-reaching implications for the legal system if this wording were to be seen as an autonomous, free standing constitutional guarantee applicable to both public and private actors alike.

---

[1]   [2017] IESC 25.

This is where the suspended declaration of unconstitutionality comes in. It was first utilised by the Supreme Court in its seminal judgment on the right to work in *NHV v Minister for Justice*[2] and it is striking that it has been utilised in the last three out of four findings of unconstitutionality delivered since that date. In *AB v Clinical Director of St. Loman's Hospital*[3] the Court of Appeal addressed the question of the suspension of a declaration of unconstitutionality saying in the context of the invalidation of provisions of the Mental Health Act 2001 providing for the long term detention of certain psychiatric patients:

> "If these patients (or any of them) were suddenly released by a judicial pronouncement of the unconstitutionality of this key sub-section of the 2001 Act, this would be likely to have unfortunate consequences for their personal welfare and might well, in some circumstances at least, to pose a possible risk to the lives and safety of others.
>
> The lesson of *NHV* is that the judiciary should not have to watch on helplessly as a finding of unconstitutionality leads on with remorseless logic to invalidate and unravel a large variety of administrative decisions, often in a chaotic and disruptive fashion and with possibly unforeseen consequences for third parties. If that were indeed the law, then there would then be a grave danger that in the words of Geoghegan J. in *A. v Governor of Mountjoy Prison* [2006] IESC 45, [2006] 4 I.R. 99 that 'judges considering the constitutionality or otherwise of enactments would be consciously or unconsciously affected by the consequences.'
>
> If post-*NHV* the immediate aftershocks of a finding of unconstitutionality can be confined and controlled by a suspension of that declaration, the Court is nonetheless obliged to afford the applicant a real remedy by providing that in due course the unconstitutional law will stand annulled. So it is here."

But, of course, without this safeguard of the suspended declaration, courts were frankly reluctant to invalidate legislation, precisely because of the very real and potentially chaotic consequences which often flowed from such a decision. A further advantage is that if legislation is found unconstitutional the courts can in effect commence a dialogue with the Oireachtas, starting a process that is likely to produce fairer and better legislation in the longer run.

Over and above all of this there is yet another reason for optimism. A

---

[2]    [2017] IESC 82.
[3]    [2018] IECA 123.

new generation of constitutional lawyers is coming forward with new analyses and insights. Their work can shine a way forward to see to it that Ireland is truly a state where the rights of all are meaningfully and effectively protected. Dr Kavanagh is one of those scholars of which I speak. Her new work — compact, immensely readable and yet comprehensive — provides the fullest introduction to a corpus of jurisprudence which is not only at once interesting and forever evolving, but it tells us much about Ireland of the past, the present and that which is as yet to come. For this — and much more besides — we can only express our gratitude.

**Gerard Hogan**,
Court of Appeal Building,
Four Courts,
Dublin 7
12th June 2018

# PREFACE

Constitutional Law forms the foundations of the Irish legal system. It sets out the rights of citizens, how the State functions and how the citizen can enforce legal rights against the State. It shapes and protects democracy as we know it and it is the bedrock of human rights law in Ireland.

This is book is designed to be an introductory text to give the reader the basic concepts and cases that shape the study of Irish Constitutional Law. Students should use this text as a bridge to the more authoritative works on the subject.

Law might be perceived as a subject that stands still by those who have not studied the subject but law is ever changing developing. Irish constitutional law is continually being shaped by both the people and interpreted by the courts. Over the next eighteen months from the publication date of this book, approximately eight referendums may take place which could change the rights of the citizens.

Constitutional law is framed by the history of the State and politics. Therefore, students with an interest in current affairs, politics and history will naturally enjoy the study of Constitutional Law. However, for those that didn't come from those academic backgrounds, the study of Constitutional Law will still be of interest as it sets out how the State runs and how citizens have rights to use against the State to promote and protect democracy.

As a student, Constitutional law was my favourite subject as it contained the basis of so many other subjects such as family law, criminal law, administrative law and property law. After many years of studying and lecturing Constitutional Law I am delighted to finally publish an introductory text to this subject which I hope will convey my love of this subject.

In Clarus Press, thanks to David McCartney for suggesting that I write this text and continuing support during project and Shane Gough for his incredible attention to detail during the typesetting process. I would like thank Mr Justice Gerard Hogan for providing a wonderful foreword to this text. I am extremely grateful to him for taking time to write it during an incredibly busy period in the Court of Appeal. In WIT, particularly, the Department of Applied Arts, thanks to my colleagues for their encouragement especially Grainne, Walter, Sinead and Ann-Marie. I would like to thank Ruth-Blandina Quinn who agreed to proof read the book and Robert for finding some obscure cases. There are also number of friends that have helped in writing this book by providing me with a social life so I didn't get completely lost in research!

Last, but most certainly not least, I would like to dedicate this book to my parents, Marie and Sean Kavanagh who have always supported me and instilled a love of learning in me from a young age and had unfailing patience in all my questions as a child.

***

Since completing the book one significant development in the ever changing constitutional law has occurred. On the 25th May 2018 the citizens of Ireland voted, by a large majority, to remove the provisions of the 8th Amendment which deals with the right to life of the unborn child from the Constitution. This also had the effect of removing the right to travel for termination services and the right to information on services.

The 8th Amendment was inserted due to campaigns to increase the constitutional protections for the unborn child in Irish law in case the courts would read in the right to terminations as a privacy right following similar moves in the US and the judgment in *McGee*. Prior to this, the prohibition on terminations was covered in the Offences against the Person Act 1861 which was identical to the UK provisions until the amendment of the legislation with the Abortion Act 1967 deviated from the original provisions (except for Northern Ireland). The *X* case in 1992 interpreted the 8th Amendment to allow for terminations in cases of a serious risk to the life of the mother. In 2013 the Protection of Life in Pregnancy Act reflected this provision in legislation.

However, it was argued by many that the provisions of the legislation and the wording of the amendment itself proved impossible for medical intervention where there was a risk to the health of the mother, where there was a fatal foetal abnormality or where the pregnancy resulted from rape or incest.

As the citizens have now voted to repeal the amendment, the Department of Health will be producing legislation to regulate terminations in Ireland. This legislation is expected to commence through the legislative process in Summer 2018.

**Dr Jennifer Kavanagh**,
College Street Campus,
Waterford Institute of Technology
18th June 2018

# TABLE OF CONTENTS

# TABLES OF CASES

# TABLES OF LEGISLATION

## Statutory Instruments

## Treaties, EU Instruments and Conventions

# CHAPTER ONE

# INTRODUCTION

"Constitutionalism—that is, the idea that the rulers are bound by rules that are not easy to change, and at certain fundamental rights of the citizens are protected absolutely, or almost absolutely—is an integral feature of contemporary liberal democracies."[1]

A Constitution is not just a legal document. It encapsulates the envisaged relationship between a State, its citizens and the rest of the world. It is also a product of the times in which it was written, while also aspiring to be a statement of the future direction of the State. The Irish Constitution is no different from this. It is also a representation of the legal, social and political climate in which it was drafted.

The Irish Constitution, or Bunreacht na hÉireann, its official name, is a written constitution which contains many of the common features of constitutions, such as delineating the organs of government and their responsibilities, and setting out the rights of the citizens. A robust constitution is designed to protect the majority from the tyranny of government. As stated by JS Mill in the celebrated work *On Liberty*[2]:

"The aim, therefore, of patriots, was to set limits to the power which the ruler should be suffered to exercise over the community; and this limitation was what they meant by liberty. It was attempted in two ways. First, by obtaining a recognition of certain immunities, called political liberties or rights, which it was to be regarded as a breach of duty in the ruler to infringe, and which if he did infringe, specific resistance, or general rebellion, was held to be justifiable. A second, and generally a later expedient, was the establishment of constitutional checks; by which the consent of the community, or of a body of some sort, supposed to represent its interests, was made a necessary condition to some of the more important acts of the governing power."[3]

The benefits of a written constitution are many, but the key benefit is the clear and accessible format in which the rules are laid down. The Irish Constitution, in comparison to other similar written legal documents, is clear to read. The constitution is written in both English and Irish with equal prominence as they are both recognised as the primary languages of the State. However, as Irish is regarded as the

---

[1]  M Gallagher, "The Changing Constitution" in J Coakley and M Gallagher, *Politics in the Republic of Ireland* (5th ed, PSAI Press, Galway, 2010), p 72.
[2]  JS Mill, *On Liberty* (JW Parker, London, 1859).
[3]  *ibid.*

first official language and English recognised as the second official language, the Irish text will prevail.[4]

The document sets out the Christian democratic nature of the State in the Preamble. This is symptomatic of the social climate in which it was drafted. It sets the boundaries of the State, both territorial, and in respect of its powers. The influence of the political climate regarding Northern Ireland and the aspirations for reunification are especially telling when considering the original drafting of Articles 2 and 3 which laid a constitutional claim to the entire Island. This was later amended in line with the provisions of the Good Friday Agreement.[5] It establishes and creates the delineations of the organs of government while it also seeks to enshrine basic rights for the citizen with the State.[6]

A constitution also has a political component, in that it sets out the democratic nature of the State and how the political institutions of the State will operate in line with the contemporary political climate of the time. It also sets out the locus of power in the State; in the Irish instance, it sets the locus of power as being from the people in the form of popular sovereignty.[7]

A constitution is the primary legal source in a country. This means that all other legal sources, such as legislation and case law, must follow the provisions contained in the constitution. The rights and duties that are set out in a constitution tend to be broad. Where further legal statements are required on issues — for example, elections which are set out in the constitution but need further legal clarification — the principles enshrined in the constitution are fleshed out in the supporting legislation which will deal with the mechanics of the process. There are a number of advantages to this approach, in that the essence of the right will be in the constitution but the mechanics which may need amendment in future can support the general statement of the right but can be amended by the parliament without the need to refer back to the citizens in a referendum. With regard to divorce in Ireland, the requirements for a divorce were enshrined in the Constitution for the very reason that amending the grounds would require reference to the citizens in a referendum.[8]

---

[4] See section 3.2 for a further discussion of language in the Constitution.
[5] See section 3.1.1.1 for a further discussion of the impact of the Good Friday Agreement on the Constitution.
[6] See chapter 7 which details the constitutional rights of the citizen.
[7] See section 3.2.2.
[8] See chapter 8 which details referendums.

CHAPTER TWO

# THE HISTORY OF THE IRISH CONSTITUTION

## 2.0 Introduction

The historical development of the Irish Constitution can be considered in four stages: the ideas of the Irish State before independence, the 1919 Constitution, the 1922 Constitution and the reasons for the creation of the current 1937 Constitution. Each stage is important, not only in the creation of the constitutional document that we have, but in developing the structures of government that were enshrined in the Irish Constitution. The historical development of the Constitution is also an important factor in the judicial interpretation of the document.[1] Murray J *obiter* in *Sinnott v Minister for Education* stated as follows:

> "Agreeing as I do with the view that the Constitution is a living document which falls to be interpreted in accordance with contemporary circumstances including prevailing ideas and mores, this does not mean, and I do not think it has ever been so suggested, that it can be divorced from its historical context. Indeed, by definition that which is contemporary is determined by reference to its historical context."[2]

The Irish State emerged from revolution. As stated by Kissane, "all revolutions are linked to the existence of fundamental norms and values which are then expressed in constitutions."[3] The same can be found in the Irish Constitution where the expression of independence is clear from the early articles in the Constitution. Also, particular rights such as freedom from arrest, within and going to or from the Houses of the Oireachtas would have been influenced by the early days of the State, in particular the first Dáil in 1919.

## 2.1 Pre-Independence

Under the Act of Union 1800, Ireland no longer had its own parliament and legislation for Ireland was passed in the parliament at Westminster. However, there were still executive government functions retained in Ireland. The constitutional framework of Ireland was part of the unwritten constitutional tradition of Westminster. At the start of the Home Rule and independence movement, the rhetoric of the leaders of the moment sought to completely distance the new State from the United Kingdom, and any form of administration connected with it. The original democratic ideal was documented by Kissane

---

[1] See interpretation of the Constitution at section 8.2.
[2] [2001] 2 IR 545 at 680.
[3] B Kissane, *New beginnings: Constitutionalism and Democracy in Modern Ireland* (UCD Press, Dublin, 2011), p xi.

in *The Constitutional Revolution That Never Was: Democratic Radicalism and the Sinn Féin Movement.*[4] This idea of democracy rejected all that was British. As per Kissane, the Sinn Féin movement believed that "as the state collapsed, this civil society would claim its place and a more organized form of democracy would emerge."[5] The emerging national identity of an independent Ireland was shaped through cultural revolution. However, there was a split in the approach to independence. The Irish Parliamentary Party sought to achieve Home Rule as a form of delegated governance through the Westminster Parliament, while the Sinn Féin party took a full independence approach. The Irish Parliamentary Party was the more politically successful party until the 1918 General Election which saw Sinn Féin take more seats and instead of travelling to Westminster, set up the first Dáil in 1919 where the first Constitution was set out.

## 2.2 1919 Constitution

Until the 1918 General Election, the Irish Parliamentary Party, which espoused Home Rule as opposed to complete independence, was the majority party representing the Irish people in Westminster. However, its electoral defeat has to be seen in the context of the failed Home Rule Bills and the failure to implement the third Home Rule Bill due to the outbreak of the First World War. One of the reasons advanced to explain the rapid electoral advantages of the militants is the failure of the British to make sufficient concessions to constitutional nationalists[6] which culminated in the 1916 Rising.

The 1919 Constitution, known as the Constitution of Dáil Éireann, was set by the first Dáil which met on 21 January 1919. This constitution did not have any legal effect, as the first Dáil was made up of the Sinn Féin members that were returned to Westminster but refused to take their seats and met in Dublin instead. The short document produced in Irish[7] set out the aspirations of an embryonic State at the brink of recognition.[8] The 1919 Constitution had five articles which set out the

---

[4] (2009) 104 *Radical History Review* 77.
[5] (2009) 104 *Radical History Review* 77 at p 86.
[6] J Coakley "The Foundations of Statehood" in J Coakley and M Gallagher, *Politics in the Republic of Ireland* (5th ed, PSAI Press, Galway, 2010), p 16.
[7] The original reading of the Constitution of Dáil Eireann can be found on the Dáil Transcript of the meeting of the First Dáil at http://oireachtasdebates. oireachtas.ie/debates%20authoring/debateswebpack.nsf/takes/ dail1919012100006?opendocument (accessed 23 September 2017).
[8] An English translation of the document can be found at http://www.difp.ie/ docs/1919/Constitution-of-Dail-Eireann/6.htm (accessed 23 September 2017) which reflects the amended version of 1 April 1919.

holding of executive power,[9] the chair of the Dáil,[10] and the budget.[11] Article 5 allowed for the variation of the 1919 Constitution. Article 1 also framed the popular sovereignty of the embryonic State which was to be reiterated throughout the Irish Constitutions that followed:

> "All legislative powers shall be vested in Dáil Éireann, composed of Deputies, elected by the Irish people from the existing Irish Parliamentary Constituencies."[12]

Even though the Constitution which emanated from this first Dáil had no legal effect, it was a declaration of aspirational independence. In the same Dáil session, the Declaration of Independence was set out.[13] This Declaration reflected the same themes as the Proclamation, such as the reference to an armed struggle for independence, the repudiation of British rule, the assertion of the Republic and allegiance to it,[14] the creation of laws for the Irish people by an Irish parliament and the references to religion as in an invocation for the future of Ireland.

## 2.3 1922 Constitution

Between the 1919 Constitution of Dáil Éireann and the Anglo–Irish Treaty, the Government of Ireland Act 1920 (the "1920 Act"), also informally known as the Fourth Home Rule Bill,[15] was passed and created the constitutional foundations of Northern Ireland. In fact, the 1920 Act continued to shape the constitutional structures of Northern Ireland until it was fully repealed as part of the Good Friday Agreement in 1998.[16] The 1920 Act was welcomed by the Unionists in Northern Ireland but was not supported in Ireland, as a War of Independence had already broken out in the wake of the First Dáil and the Declaration of Independence in 1919.

---

9   Art 2 of the Constitution of Dáil Éireann 1919.
10  Art 3 of the Constitution of Dáil Éireann 1919.
11  Art 4 of the Constitution of Dáil Éireann 1919.
12  Art 1 of the Constitution of Dáil Éireann 1919.
13  Declaration of Independence in *Minutes and Proceedings of the First Dáil of the Republic of Ireland 1919–1921* (Dublin, 1994), available at http://www.difp.ie/docs/volume/1/1919/1.htm (accessed 23 September 2017).
14  Though note the discussion in section 3.2 on Nation and State regarding the use of the word "Republic" in the name of the State.
15  The first Home Rule Bill in 1886 was defeated by the House of Commons. The second Home Rule Bill in 1893 was passed by the House of Commons but vetoed by the House of Lords. The third Home Rule Bill in 1914 was passed and given Royal Assent in 1914 but did not come into force due to the outbreak of the First World War.
16  See the discussion related to Northern Ireland in chapter 3 on Nation and State, particularly section 3.1.1.

The 1922 Constitution, which was formally known as the Constitution of the Irish Free State or Bunreacht Shaorstáit Éireann, originated from the provisions of the Anglo–Irish Treaty of 1922 (the "Treaty"). The Constitution of the Irish Free State was the first constitution to have legal effect. The constitution was promulgated into law as the Constitution of the Irish Free State (Saorstát Éireann) Act 1922. The First Schedule of the Act contained the Constitution, and the Second Schedule contained the Treaty. The Annex to the Act contained provisions relating to the treaty ports,[17] fuel storage by these ports, and a convention dealing with submarine cables, lighthouses and war signal stations.

The 1922 Constitution asserted Ireland's independence but also its membership of the British Commonwealth of Nations. Many of the provisions of the 1922 Constitution are similar in both wording and effect to their provisions in the 1937 Constitution. However, there was a number of articles which reflected the dominion status of Ireland and retained the power of the British monarchy in Ireland due to its membership of the Commonwealth. In Art 17, members of the Oireachtas had to swear an oath of allegiance to the Crown.[18] Under Art 41, there had to be royal assent for any legislation passed by the Oireachtas.[19] Article 51 vested executive power in the King.[20] Article 60 created the office of Governor General to represent the power of the Crown in Ireland.[21] The representative of the Crown had the power to appoint judges under Art 68.[22] The Constitution establishes the forms of executive governance that were recognisable to the United Kingdom. In fact, commentators such as Neil Collins state that the "Irish Free State inherited an almost complete administrative system".[23] The Treaty offered full internal self-government to Ireland, financial autonomy and the right to its own police and army under the control of the parliament. It conferred dominion status on Ireland, which in 1921 was a new and undefined concept. However, it created Northern Ireland. This Treaty was to be the catalyst to the Irish Civil War. The 1922 Constitution was to formalise Westminster and Whitehall governance structures in Ireland. This is why the Oireachtas and the government have shared characteristics with their UK counterparts.

---

[17] Dockyard Port at Berehaven (Castletownbere and Bere Island in Cork), Queenstown (Spike Island near Cobh), Belfast Lough and Lough Swilly (Donegal). Berehaven, Queenstown and Lough Swilly were handed back to the Irish government in 1938 after the Anglo–Irish Trade War.

[18] Art 17 of Constitution of the Irish Free State (Saorstát Éireann) Act 1922.

[19] Art 41 of Constitution of the Irish Free State (Saorstát Éireann) Act 1922.

[20] Art 51 of Constitution of the Irish Free State (Saorstát Éireann) Act 1922.

[21] Art 60 of Constitution of the Irish Free State (Saorstát Éireann) Act 1922.

[22] Art 68 of Constitution of the Irish Free State (Saorstát Éireann) Act 1922.

[23] N Collins, "Parliamentary Democracy in Ireland" (2004) 57(3) *Parliamentary Affairs* 601 at p 601.

The 1922 Constitution also set out the basic fundamental rights of the citizen in the new Irish Free State.

## 2.4 Factors Leading up to the 1937 Constitution

A number of legal issues and political issues would shape the 1922 Constitution into an unworkable document and create the need for a revised constitution within 14 years of the 1922 Constitution coming into force. Several minor changes were made to that Constitution, but there were also sweeping changes which interfered with the fundamental rights enshrined in the 1922 Constitution and further, a gradual undermining of the Treaty provisions contained in the original document.

In all, there were 27 amendments to the Constitution of the Irish Free State. The first amendment of the 1922 Constitution amended the terms of office of Senators.[24] There were also a number of procedural amendments to the Constitution, such as the increase of members of the Executive Council, now referred to as the cabinet,[25] the establishment of the practice of automatically returning the Ceann Comhairle to the Dáil in an election[26] and the replacement of the direct election system for the Seanad with an indirect system.[27]

The Constitution (Amendment No 10) Act 1928 removed the provisions for direct democracy in the Constitution. Direct democracy was a key feature of the envisaged constitution of the early framers of the Irish State.[28] Article 47 of the 1922 Constitution allowed for a Bill to be referred to the people if there was a successful petition of one-twentieth of the electorate.[29] The 10th Amendment also removed Art 48 of the Constitution. This Article, as per the text itself, was to "provide for the Initiation by the people of proposals for laws or constitutional amendments".[30] The effect of this Article would have been to fully enshrine direct democracy in Ireland where by

"petition of not less than seventy five thousand voters on the

---

[24] Constitution (Amendment No 1) Act 1925.
[25] Constitution (Amendment No 5) Act 1927.
[26] Constitution (Amendment No 2) Act 1927.
[27] Constitution (Amendment No 6) Act 1928.
[28] See the section 5.3 detailing the role of the cabinet in the 1937 Constitution and section 2.4 relating to the cabinet in the 1922 Constitution.
[29] The census figures for Ireland in the 1926 Census show a population of around 3 million. Therefore, just under 150,000 signatures would have been needed to activate this provision. See http://census.ie/in-history/population-of-ireland-1841-2006/ (accessed 25/08/17).
[30] Art 47 of Constitution of the Irish Free State (Saorstát Éireann) Act 1922.

register, of whom not more than fifteen thousand shall be voters in any one constituency, either make such provisions or submit the question to the people for decision"[31].

This was a major change to Treaty enshrined provisions.

The 16th Amendment of the 1922 Constitution in 1929[32] extended the provision to allow for amendments to the Constitution to be carried out by ordinary legislation from eight years to sixteen years. A provision to amend a constitution by means of ordinary legislation is common to new constitutions to allow for a period of reflection and minor amendment without the need for referenda.[33] In the 1922 Constitution, it allowed many amendments to be made which may not have passed a referendum if it were left to the electorate to determine their merits for inclusion in the Constitution. The Cumann na nGaedheal government of the time were fearful that the anti-Treaty Fianna Fáil party would use these provisions to undermine the Constitution, and thereby the Anglo–Irish Treaty.

The 16th Amendment of the Constitution also paved the way for the insertion of Art 2A[34] into the Constitution. It was introduced by the Constitution (Amendment No 17) Act 1931 as part of an "infatuation with draconian security powers".[35] The long title of the Act states that its purpose was to prevent disorder by means of establishing wide-ranging security mechanisms to curb terrorist activities at the time. The Schedule to the Act sets out special military tribunals, special powers for the Gardaí and provisions dealing with unlawful associations, and the final section includes miscellaneous powers with important implications for constitutional rights, such as searches and restrictions on freedom of expression.

Notwithstanding those major changes to the constitutional framework of the 1922 document, the most sweeping changes came in the period between 1933–1936. By this stage, the Cumann na nGaedheal party had governed the State from the pro-Treaty members of the first Dáil and formed the first governments from 1923 to 1932. During the early years of the Irish parliament, or Oireachtas, the anti-Treaty members of Sinn Féin, and later, Fianna Fáil, were not in opposition to Cumann na nGaedheal in parliament, as they refused to take the oath of allegiance

---

[31] Art 48 of Constitution of the Irish Free State (Saorstát Éireann) Act 1922.

[32] Constitution (Amendment No 16) Act 1929.

[33] The plural for referendum for different measures is referendums whereas the plural for referendum on the same issue is referenda.

[34] Constitution (Amendment No 6) Act 1928.

[35] P Martin, *Censorship in the Two Irelands 1922–1939* (Irish Academic Press, Dublin, 2006), p 124.

under the 1922 Constitution. Under the provisions of s 4(2) of the Electoral (Amendment) Act 1927, all members of the Oireachtas were forced to take the oath, or else they would be disqualified from being a member of the Oireachtas, so the returned Fianna Fáil members were forced to take their seats. Fianna Fáil was returned as the largest party in the Dáil in the 1932 general election, and set about dismantling the remaining vestiges of British rule which were part of the 1922 Constitution through a number of amendments.

The first symbol of British rule which was removed was an Oath of Allegiance in the Constitution (Removal of Oath) Act 1933. Considering that the oath had prevented previous members from taking their seats, and was forced upon them eventually through legislation, this was an obvious target for the Fianna Fáil government. The next amendments curtailed the power of the Governor General by first removing its role in the budget-making process for the State,[36] and then removing its role in the vetoing of legislation or the referral of legislation to London.[37] The position of Governor General itself was abolished by constitutional amendment in 1936.[38] The right of appeal to the Privy Council was also removed to ensure that the Irish State had full control over its own judiciary, and the Supreme Court of the Irish Free State was established as the final court of appeal in Ireland.[39]

The final two amendments made during this time period altered representation to the Dáil and abolished the Seanad. The university constituencies which had representation in the Dáil were abolished.[40] Article 27 entitled each of the three universities in Ireland at the time of independence to elect three representatives each to the Dáil, mirroring parliamentary representation in the House of Commons that had been in place prior to independence.[41]

The Seanad was abolished in 1936 in the Constitution (Amendment No 24) Act 1936. This legislation repealed 16 articles of the original 1922 Constitution and fundamentally changed the parliamentary structures in the Constitution. The eventual scheme of the Seanad which was reinstated in the later 1937 Constitution was a weaker body than the original Seanad envisaged in the 1922 Constitution.[42]

---

[36] Constitution (Amendment No 20) Act 1933.
[37] Constitution (Amendment No 21) Act 1933.
[38] Constitution (Amendment No 27) Act 1936.
[39] Constitution (Amendment No 22) Act 1933.
[40] Constitution (Amendment No 23) Act 1936.
[41] For example, Edward Carson, one of the leaders of Unionism in Ireland, was elected to the House of Commons from the Dublin University (Trinity College) constituency.
[42] For example, in the 1922 Seanad structure there were no members appointed

In May 1935, Taoiseach Eamon de Valera signalled that a new Constitution would be created. However, in 1936, the abdication of King Edward VIII provided the Irish government with the means of removing all mention of the Crown and dominion from the internal workings of Irish democracy. Hogan and Whyte state that the position of the King in the 1922 Constitution was hidden: "The King survived only in a hidden form—like a face camouflaged by foliage in a children's puzzle—namely in a new sentence".[43]

The creation of a new constitution was a radical move of itself, as the 1922 Constitution did not envisage its own replacement by another document—it was a legal agreement for the independence of Ireland from the United Kingdom. However, with these aims achieved without the need for a new constitution, there was still a requirement for a new document. There were also legal reasons requiring the need for a new complete document.

The legal reasons for requiring a new Constitution were set out in two cases: *Moore v Attorney General*[44] and *State (Ryan) v Lennon*.[45] Both cases examined the legality of the constitutional amendments that were carried out to the 1922 Constitution, the impact of the changes on the provisions of the Anglo–Irish Treaty and the continued legitimacy of the 1922 Constitution.

In *Moore v Attorney General*,[46] the constitutionality of the removal of the Oath of Allegiance and the removal of the Privy Council right of appeal were challenged. The core consideration was whether these amendments to the Constitution were valid, considering the Statute of Westminster 1939 and the ability of the Constitution to be amended past the eight-year time period by means of extending this time limit by ordinary legislation. This position was summed up in the judgment of Viscount Sankey LC of the Judicial Committee as follows:

> "The simplest way of stating the situation is to say that the Statute of Westminster gave to the Irish Free State a power under which they could abrogate the Treaty, and that, as a matter of law, they have availed themselves of that power."[47]

---

by the Taoiseach. Whereas the Taoiseach of the day appoints 11 members in the current Seanad format.

43   G Hogan and G Whyte, *JM Kelly: The Irish Constitution* (4th ed, Tottel Publishing, Dublin, 2006), p 2112.

44   [1935] 1 IR 473; see also *State (Attorney General) v Shaw* [1979] IR 136 for a similar consideration of the removal of Crown symbolism from the 1922 Constitution.

45   [1935] IR 170.

46   [1935] 1 IR 473.

47   *ibid* at 487.

The case of *State (Ryan) v Lennon*[48] focused on the broad powers that were handed to Special Military Tribunals to deal with internal disorder in the State by inserting Art 2A into the 1922 Constitution. Both the High Court and the Supreme Court upheld the constitutionality of the provisions but there was a very strong dissenting judgment from the Chief Justice.

The arguments focused on the validity of Art 2A and the means of its insertion into the Constitution. First, that the mechanism used to insert Art 2A itself was flawed, in that the extension of the amendment of the Constitution from eight years to sixteen years by ordinary legislation was not compatible with Art 50. Essentially, it was argued that the government was acting *ultra vires* by amending the Constitution in such a manner. This was also commented upon by the Chief Justice in his exceptionally strong dissenting opinion,[49] including the range of powers that could be exercised when Art 2A came into force[50] and the effect on the separation of powers doctrine.[51]

Secondly, it was argued that the erosion of fundamental rights in the Constitution by Art 2A was unconstitutional, as the rights themselves were so fundamental to the spirit of the entire Constitution that the provisions of Art 2A could not remove them. This could be summed up as a natural law argument regarding fundamental rights.[52]

By not stating the fundamental rights of the citizen in the 1922 Constitution in terms of inalienable rights, there was no argument to say that there were fundamental rights in the Constitution of Dáil Éireann that were fettered or rendered redundant by the provisions of Art 2A. The essence of the judgment upholding the provisions of Art 2A, and its method of insertion, can be summarised by the following excerpt from the judgment of Fitzgibbon J:

> "The framers of our Constitution may have intended

---

[48] [1935] IR 170.

[49] *ibid* at 195.

[50] *ibid* at 197. For example, Kennedy CJ states "the more one dwells on this paragraph, the more one is staggered by the contemplation of the range of its operation and the scope of the matter is authorised by it". Additionally "in general it may be said that some of the provisions to which I have been referring are the antithesis of the rule of law, and are, within their scope, the rule of anarchy." [1935] IR 170 at 198.

[51] [1935] IR 170 at 202 "The net effect, then, is that the Oireachtas has taken a judicial power from the Judiciary and handed it to the Executive and has surrendered its own trust to the Legislature to the Executive Council, in respect of the extensive area of matters covered by the Appendix to the Article".

[52] See Kennedy CJ's statement on the natural law elements at [1935] 1 IR 170, 205.

'to bind man down from mischief by the chains of the Constitution,' but if they did, they defeated their object by handing him the key of the padlock in Article 50."[53]

## 2.5 Continuity between Constitutions

Both the 1922 Constitution and the current 1937 Constitution have provisions in place for the continuity of laws between constitutional periods. These aspects are key to the validity of constitutions and the continued validity of laws.[54]

The transitory provisions for the coming into operation of the Constitution of the Irish Free State are set out in Arts 73–83. They are longer than the provisions that were required for the transition between the 1922 and 1937 constitutions, but this is understandable, as the change from British Rule to independence was more fundamental and wide reaching than the transition between two constitutional documents.

Article 73 states that legislation in force prior to the 1937 Constitution coming into operation will continue with legal power unless they are inconsistent with the provisions of the Constitution.[55] Article 74 dealt with taxation issues and stated that goods transported from or to Ireland from Great Britain or the Isle of Man would not be treated as exports or imports,[56] unless otherwise directed by the Executive Council. Article 75 continued with the courts' structure that was in place at the time of the establishment of the Irish Free State and stated that judges would continue in their office unless they resigned.[57] Articles 77 to 79 dealt with the continuation of the civil service and the transfer of the administration of any public service that it was not already providing to the Provisional government. Article 80 stated that departmental property, assets, rights and liabilities were to be transferred to the Free State government as successors to the Provisional government and that the Free State government would take over functions of the British government. Article 81 dealt with

---

[53] [1935] 1 IR 170 at 235.
[54] See further A Keating "The Validity of a Constitution' (2012) 30 ILT 246–248.
[55] An example of incompatibility in the 1937 constitutional landscape was the failed application of the Royal Prerogative of Treasure Trove in *Webb v Ireland* [1988] 1 IR 353 and see the discussion in section 3.2 on the issue of the State and mineral right and also see section 2.6 on the issue of the validity of laws promulgated before the 1937 Constitution. See also *Byrne v Ireland* [1972] IR 241 regarding the non-survival of prerogative rights in the Constitution.
[56] Though this was to change with the Anglo–Irish Trade War which was to follow.
[57] Further provisions regarding judges were made in Art 76.

the transitory arrangements for the Dáil. Article 82 dealt with the transitory provisions for the creation of the Seanad and the election of its members by both appointment by the Executive Council and election from the Dáil. The final article in the transitory provisions, Art 83, dealt with the communication of the passage and adoption of the Constitution, the issuing of a proclamation to that effect by the King and that the Constitution would come into operation once the proclamation was issued.

The level of detail required for the handover of political, legal and administrative power was essential in the 1922 Constitution as it was created as part of the Anglo-Irish Treaty which granted Ireland its independence. To ensure the continuity of laws, there had to be a clear rooting of political and legal power within the document itself to ensure that Ireland was granted the power to be a sovereign, independent and democratic nation. The continuity of laws, the first element of the transitory powers, was essential. It was formulated in a way that preserved the laws in force at the time of the operation of the Constitution, as the creation of a completely new legal and legislative landscape for the new State would have been an insurmountable challenge for a new State and it would have removed any semblance of certainty in the administration of law.

In *Exham v Beamish*[58] Gavan Duffy J considered the issue of the continuation of laws from pre-independence to the 1922 Constitution and summarised the position concisely and clearly as follows:

> "As a matter of practice, we constantly refer to judgments in the English Courts and such judgments, as every lawyer will recognise, have often proved to be of great service to us; but let us be clear. In my opinion, when Saorstát Éireann, and afterwards Éire, continued the laws in force, they did not make binding on their Courts anything short of law. In my opinion, judicial decisions in Ireland before the Treaty, and English decisions which were followed here, are binding upon this Court only when they represent a law so well settled or pronounced by so weighty a juristic authority that they may fairly be regarded, in a system built up upon the principle of stare decisis, as having become established as part of the law of the land before the Treaty; and to bind, they must, of course, not be inconsistent with the Constitution."[59]

---

[58] [1939] IR 336.
[59] *ibid* at 348.

This very section was quoted with approval by Davitt P in *The State (Quinn) v Ryan*[60]:

> "If this matter had to be decided according to common law and apart from the provisions of Article 40 of the Constitution, then, having regard to all the circumstances … represents a principle (of common law) so well settled, or pronounced by so weighty a juristic authority, that it became part of the law under the combined operation of Article 73 of the Constitution of 1922 and Article 50 of the present Constitution. I would take the view that this Court was free to accept, reject, modify or ignore that principle as we see fit."[61]

## 2.6 Repeal of the 1922 Constitution

Articles 48–50 of the 1937 Constitution dealt with the repeal of the 1922 Constitution to ensure that there was a clear process for the continuation of laws. As there was a complete and effective political and legal system in the jurisdiction that was 'Irish', the provision for the continuity of laws was not as strictly legislated as with the transitory provisions contained in the 1922 Constitution. Article 48 establishes that the 1922 Constitution will be repealed from the date that the 1937 Constitution comes into effect. Article 49 vests all "powers, functions, rights and prerogatives"[62] that were exercisable by the Free State in the people and stated that they can only be exercised by the government or on the authority of the government established by the 1937 Constitution. This Article also states that the government established by the 1937 Constitution is the successor of the government of Saorstát Éireann regarding all "property, assets, rights and liabilities".[63] The final Article in the repeal of the 1922 Constitution deals with the continuity of laws from the 1922 Constitution following the same provision regarding compatibility as stated in the transitory provisions section of the 1922 Constitution.

---

[60] [1965] IR 70.
[61] *ibid* at 88.
[62] Art 49.2 Bunreacht na hÉireann.
[63] Art 48.3 Bunreacht na hÉireann.

---

# DEFINING THE NATION AND STATE

---

## 3.0 Introduction

Ireland is an international legal actor and, as such sets out its right to sovereignty, territory, symbols and democratic nature in Arts 1 through to 11. This chapter splits the consideration of nation and State along the lines of the Constitution itself. Bearing in mind that at the time the Constitution was drafted in 1936, the issue of Northern Ireland was both a legal and political challenge. The main focus of this section is on the content and impact of Arts 1–11 but it will also look at the provisions of Art 29 which focus on Ireland and international relations. The idea of the nation and the State is encompassed in Arts 1–11. The provisions of Arts 2 and 3 were changed by reason of Irish commitments under the Good Friday Agreement 1998, also known as the Belfast Agreement.

## 3.1 The Nation

Article 1 sets out the sovereignty of the Irish State in terms of an inalienable, indefeasible, and sovereign right to self-government and international relations. Hogan and Whyte state that this construction was based on a theory of nationalism.[1] This formulation also informed the jurisprudence of the court in *McGimpsey v Ireland*, where the claim to the six counties of Northern Ireland under the provisions of the old Arts 2 and 3 of the Constitution was determined to be a right rather than a political claim.[2] Sovereignty is an important part of international law and statehood in that a country is deemed to have the ability to govern itself and be independent and equal to other countries. Article 1 states that

> "The Irish nation hereby affirms its inalienable, indefeasible, and sovereign right to choose its own form of Government, to determine its relations with other nations, and to develop its life, political, economic and cultural, in accordance with its own genius and traditions."

This article clearly signals the independence of the nation in both its internal and external governance. It is a clear signal to the history of the country that it is now independent and will be driven by its own cultural traditions.

---

[1]  G Hogan and G Whyte, *JM Kelly: The Irish Constitution* (4th ed, Tottel Publishing, Dublin, 2006).

[2]  [1990] 1 IR 110.

### 3.1.1 Articles 2 and 3–The Historical Significance

The old formulation of Articles 2 and 3 is as follows:

> "Article 2
> The national territory consists of the whole island of Ireland, its islands and the territorial sea
>
> Article 3
> Pending the re-integration of the national territory, and without prejudice to the right of the Parliament and Government established by the Constitution to exercise jurisdiction over the whole of that territory, the laws enacted by that Parliament shall have the like area and extend of application as the law of Saorstát Éireann and the like extra-territorial effect."

Considering that the six counties of Ulster which still comprise of Northern Ireland were under the direct control of the United Kingdom, in *McGimpsey v Ireland*,[3] the Supreme Court held that the former Art 3 was a claim as of right and not just a political claim. This case was taken on the basis of the Anglo–Irish Agreement of 1985 which included a provision affirming the existing status of Northern Ireland and that any change to this position would only happen with the consent of the majority of the population of Northern Ireland. The agreement also included provisions to establish an intergovernmental conference and to allow the Irish government to put forward its views on devolution and major legislative and policy proposals within Northern Ireland in relation to the interests of the minority community in Northern Ireland. The agreement also included other provisions related to security and legal matters, cross border co-operation and economic development. The plaintiff argued that this agreement was contrary to Arts 2 and 3 as it prevented the State from enforcing its right to Northern Ireland under international law. This argument was rejected by the court, but the judgment is notable in that it interprets the claim to Northern Ireland as a right as follows:

> "The conclusion that these articles of the Anglo–Irish Agreement do not constitute any form of abandonment of the claim of right to the re-integration of the national territory but constitute instead a realistic recognition of the *de facto* situation in Northern Ireland leads to the consequential conclusion that the Anglo–Irish Agreement cannot be impugned on the basis of any supposed estoppel arising to

---

3   [1990] 1 IR 110.

defeat the constitutional claim to re-integration, nor on the basis of any indefinite duration in the Agreement."[4]

Any argument that had been put forward by the government that the claim to Northern Ireland was merely a political aspiration stemming from the constitutional and political history in which the State was founded could not continue. This had the effect of placing the status of the old Articles 2 and 3 firmly in the remit of a constitutional right.

The court accepted that both governments of the UK and Ireland have an acknowledged concern in relation to the affairs of Northern Ireland and it "acknowledges that the Government of Ireland may make representations, put forward proposals, and try to influence the evolution of peace and order in Northern Ireland".[5] Therefore as part of the peace process, Ireland agreed to relinquish its claim on Northern Ireland and hence this proposal was agreed to by the population by means of referendum.

### 3.1.1.1 Good Friday Agreement

Under Art 4 of the Good Friday Agreement,[6] the Irish government agreed to amend Arts 2 and 3 of the Irish constitution. The current provisions of these Articles reflect the agreement of the parties. As part of the Agreement, the Irish government also committed to adding this Agreement to the international relations section of the Constitution as per amendment to Art 29.7. The provisions of the Good Friday Agreement also instituted the Northern Irish Assembly in Stormont, the importance of the baseline standard of the European Convention on Human Rights across Ireland, Northern Ireland and the United Kingdom, and the Northern Irish Executive. To ensure joint supervision of the Northern Irish political bodies through the Good Friday Agreement, the document also establishes the North/South Ministerial Council, the British–Irish Council, and the British–Irish

---

[4]   *McGimpsey v Ireland* [1990] 1 IR 110, 121.

[5]   *ibid* at 121. Interestingly, Finlay CJ also stated the following with regard to the re-integration of the North: "I would also point out, however, that there is, looking at the Anglo–Irish Agreement in its totality and looking at the entire scheme and thrust of the Constitution of Ireland a high improbability that a clear attempt to resolve the position with regard to the re-integration of the national territory and the position of Northern Ireland by a process of consultation, discussion and reasoned argument structured by constant communication between servants of each of the two states concerned could ever be inconsistent with a Constitution devoted to the ideals of ordered, peaceful international relations" *McGimpsey v Ireland* [1990] 1 IR 110 at 121.

[6]   The full text of the Good Friday Agreement can be found at https://www.dfa.ie/media/dfa/alldfawebsitemedia/ourrolesandpolicies/northernireland/good-friday-agreement.pdf (accessed 9 February 2018).

Intergovernmental Conference. Such moves were incorporated in the Sunningdale Agreement of 1973 and the Anglo–Irish Agreement of 1985. The Good Friday Agreement contains provisions for remedial action where difficulties arise which include consultation with all parties and the two governments.

### 3.1.1.2 The Current Approach and Challenges

The original Arts 2 and 3 were replaced with Art 2 which based the nation on nationality, which was to be subject to qualification in law, and was altered by the 27th Amendment of the Constitution in 2004. The post-Good Friday Agreement version included the *jus soli* claim to citizenship. This concept refers to an unqualified right to citizenship for those born in Ireland. The current formulation of Articles 2 and 3 is as follows:

> "Article 2
> It is the entitlement and birthright of every person born in the island of Ireland, which includes its islands and seas, to be part of the Irish Nation. That is also the entitlement of all persons otherwise qualified in accordance with law to be citizens of Ireland. Furthermore, the Irish nation cherishes its special affinity with people of Irish ancestry living abroad who share its cultural identity and heritage.

> Article 3
> 1 It is the firm will of the Irish Nation, in harmony and friendship, to unite all the people who share the territory of the island of Ireland, in all the diversity of their identities and traditions, recognising that a united Ireland shall be brought about only by peaceful means with the consent of a majority of the people, democratically expressed, in both jurisdictions in the island. Until then, the laws enacted by the Parliament established by this Constitution shall have the like area and extent of application as the laws enacted by the Parliament that existed immediately before the coming into operation of this Constitution.

> 2 Institutions with executive powers and functions that are shared between those jurisdictions may be established by their respective responsible authorities for stated purposes and may exercise powers and functions in respect of all or any part of the island."

There have been two main consequences stemming from the new

formulation: first, with regard to citizenship,[7] and secondly, the consent principle of re-integration. The legal agreement between the UK government and the Irish government specifically includes a mechanism for the re-integration of Northern Ireland into Ireland as it recognised that it is for the people of the island of Ireland to exercise their right of self-determination on the basis of consent "freely and concurrently given, North and South to bring about a united Ireland" where a "substantial section of the people in Northern Ireland share the legitimate wish of a majority of the people".[8] Therefore, if there is to be a united Ireland there must be a democratic majority vote of the people both North and South of the border to create such a united Ireland. This is reflected in Art 3.

The current issue of the UK leaving the EU under the provisions of Art 50 of the EU Treaty, generally known as "Brexit", poses difficulties for the Good Friday Agreement. Throughout the document, the EU and the European Convention on Human Rights is mentioned and the legal agreement reached between the governments of the UK and Ireland specifically references the relationship of both parties as "friendly neighbours and partners in the European Union". Furthermore, a significant number of those living in Northern Ireland hold Irish passports and their position post-Brexit could be complicated.

## 3.2 The State

The concept of the State in the Constitution is dealt with in Arts 4 through to 11 with some articles being clear and others signifying more complex democratic structures, concepts and institutions. The most straightforward articles deal with the symbols, language and name. Article 4 states that the official name for the country is Éire or in English, Ireland. The country is not officially known as a Republic. However, the Republic of Ireland Act 1948 declares that the State shall be described as a Republic. In *Ellis v O'Dea (No.1)*[9] the Supreme Court held that this did not have the effect of changing the name of the State, as only a referendum could be held to make this change. Article 7 declares the national flag of Ireland.

Article 8 states that the Irish language is the primary language of the State, English is second and that provision can be made for the exclusive use of either language for official purposes. The constitutional consideration of the official use of Irish falls under two aspects: the use

---

[7] See the discussion of citizenship in section 3.2.1.1.
[8] Sections ii and iii of the Legal Agreement between the UK government and Irish government contained in the Good Friday Agreement.
[9] [1989] IR 530.

of Irish in public services and the right to use Irish in official business such as court proceedings.

Relating to the use of Irish in court proceedings, legal notices should be available in Irish, as considered in *Attorney General v Coyne and Wallace*[10] and later in *Ó Beoláin v Fahey*.[11] In *Ó Beoláin*, the State had not provided an Irish translation of most Acts since 1980. In this case the applicant was being prosecuted under the Road Traffic Acts in the District Court and sought Irish translations of the respective Acts and the Rules of the District Court. The central question that concerned the court was the allowance of a reasonable time for translation of Acts of the Oireachtas. McGuinness J stated that the Article envisages a rapid translation process, which is not in line with a delay of over 20 years in the translation of documents; this could not be considered reasonable.[12] Hardiman J held that the "grave shortfall" in the translation of documents could "only be described as a failure to observe the constitutional imperative" in Art 8.[13]

In *An Stát (Mac Fhearraigh) v Mac Gamhna*,[14] an applicant before an Employment Appeals Tribunal not only wished to conduct his case through Irish but also sought to cross-examine witnesses in Irish. The Tribunal turned down the request but the High Court allowed for the application and in the judgment O'Hanlon J stated that the formulation of Art 8 accorded a higher status to the official use of Irish than the old Art 4. However, the provisions of Art 8 do not create a situation where a plaintiff who wishes to conduct his trial through Irish can insist on all members of the jury being able to understand without the use of a translator. This point was set in *MacCárthaigh v Éire*.[15]

The provisions of the Official Languages Act 2003 further enforced this provision regarding the recognition of the Irish language by public bodies. Prior to the enactment of the Official Languages Act 2003 a defendant was not able to insist on being served with an Irish version of a summons.[16] The primary objective of the Official Languages Act is to ensure that there is a legislative framework to improve provision of public services through Irish and to ensure that there is translation of

---

[10] (1967) 101 ILTR 17.
[11] [2001] 2 IR 279.
[12] [2001] 2 IR 279 at 307–308.
[13] [2001] 2 IR 279 at 344.
[14] [1980–1998] TÉ (Tuairiscí Speisialta) 29, [1980–1998] IR (Special Reports) 99.
[15] [1999] 1 IR 279.
[16] *An Stát (Mac Fhearraigh) v Mac Gamhna* [1980–1998] TÉ (Tuairiscí Speisialta) 29, [1980–1998] IR (Special Reports) 99. *Cf. Ó Foghludha v McLean* [1934] IR 469 — which was the only case decided under framework of the 1922 Constitutional provisions—which stated that documents served in Irish were to be accompanied with an English translation.

official documents into Irish in a timely fashion in the wake of the Ó *Beoláin*[17] case. The Act also created the Office of An Coimisinéir Teanga which was established in 2004 to monitor compliance by public bodies with the provisions of the legislation and take appropriate measures in cases of non- compliance.

Article 10 of the Constitution deals with the natural resources of the jurisdiction and the collection of royalties from exploration and mining. It covers the continuation of ownership of such resources from the previous Constitution. It also provides for the management of State property and the management of land, mines, minerals and waters. The scope of Art 10 in relation to cultural artefacts and finds was considered in the seminal case of *Webb v Ireland*[18] where a number of parties, including the State, sought ownership of the Derrynaflan Hoard. This had been found by the applicants and they sought to recover the chalice from the National Museum. The State asserted a right to own the objects found by the applicants under the Crown prerogative of treasure trove, but the applicants sought a finder's fee for locating the Hoard. Finlay CJ used the provisions of Art 10 as a replacement for the Crown prerogative of treasure trove, which was inconsistent with the provisions of the Constitution,[19] as a means of vesting ownership of the archaeological find in the State:

> "It would, I think, now be universally accepted, certainly by the People of Ireland, and by the people of most modern states, that one of the most important national assets belonging to the people is their heritage and knowledge of its true origins and the buildings and objects which constitute keys to their ancient history. If this be so, then it would appear to me to follow that a necessary ingredient of sovereignty in a modern state and certainly in this State, having regard to the terms of the Constitution, with an emphasis on its historical origins and a constant concern for the common good is and should be an ownership by the State of objects which constitute antiquities of importance which are discovered and which have no known owner. It would appear to me to be inconsistent with the framework of the society sought to be created and sought to be protected by the Constitution that such objects should become the exclusive property of those who by chance may find them.

---

17  [2001] 2 IR 279.
18  [1988] IR 353.
19  See *Byrne v Ireland* [1972] IR 241 previously for a consideration of the use and application of Crown prerogatives in the State.

The existence of such a general ingredient of the sovereignty of the State, does, however, seem to me to lead to the conclusion that the much more limited right of the prerogative of treasure trove known to the common law should be upheld not as a right derived from the Crown but rather as an inherent attribute of the sovereignty of the State which was recognised and declared by Article 11 of the 1922 Constitution.

For the purpose of determining the issues in this case, therefore, I would conclude that there does exist in the State a right or prerogative of treasure trove, the characteristics of which are the characteristics of the prerogative of treasure trove at common law which I have already outlined in this judgment as they stood in 1922.

As I have already indicated, it would appear that the characteristics of the right or prerogative of treasure trove at common law included the practice of rewarding a diligent and honest finder who revealed his find and yielded the object of it to the Crown. This practice is, however, apparently established as one of grace only and not as conferring a legal right enforceable by the courts."[20]

Article 11 allows for State revenues to be collected and placed in one fund which shall be "appropriated for purposes and in the manner and subject to the charges and liabilities determined and imposed by the law." This Article gives legal effect to the collection of revenue and its expenditure which is detailed in the yearly budget. Therefore, any application for judicial review, where the applicant is not only seeking to enforce their constitutional rights against the State but also seeking funding to secure this right, will fail as the courts have no ability to direct the legislature to spend money on the pursuit of this aim and this would be contrary to the doctrine of the separation of powers.[21]

### 3.2.1 Citizenship

Section 3 of the 1922 Constitution stated that all persons domiciled in the area of the jurisdiction of the Free State at the coming into effect of the Constitution would be citizens of Ireland. A similar provision is found in Art 9 of the 1937 Constitution which maintained citizenship between Constitutions. The *ius soli* doctrine is a common feature of

---

[20] [1988] IR 353, 383–384.
[21] An example of this would be in the *Sinnott* case ([2001] 2 IR 545) which will be discussed later in the consideration of the separation of powers in section 5.1.

common law countries. *Ius soli* means that persons born on the land of a particular State receive citizenship of that particular State. This was expressly followed in Ireland in s 6(1) of the Irish Nationality and Citizenship Act 1959.[22] The Article further states that the acquisition and loss of Irish citizenship is an issue to be determined by law and no person may be excluded on the basis of their sex.

The issue of the *ius soli* doctrine was raised in the case of *Lobe v Minister for Justice*,[23] where the revised framing of the concept of the Nation and the State had been revised in the Good Friday Agreement and inserted by referendum. In *Chen v Secretary of State for the Home Department*,[24] a non-EU national sought a right to reside in the UK on the basis that her Belfast-born child with Irish citizenship was entitled to reside in Ireland acted to increase the perception that the revised wording of Art 3 allowed for non-EU migrants to remain in Ireland through their children acquiring Irish citizenship.

On consideration of the revised article in *Lobe,* the impact in *Chen,* and the perception that these provisions were encouraging migrants to come to Ireland in order to have children who would be Irish citizens,[25] the acquisition of Irish citizenship was limited to children with at least one parent who is an Irish citizen or one parent who is entitled to be an Irish citizen.[26]

Additionally, the provisions of Art 9.2 state that "fidelity of the nation and loyalty to the State are fundamental political duties of all citizens". This was further outlined by in the *locus standi* arguments in *McGimpsey v Ireland*[27] where McCarthy J referenced the duty of citizens under the Constitution in the following terms where the trial judge concluded that each of the plaintiffs was a citizen of Ireland. As citizens they are bound by the provisions of Art 9, s 2 of the Constitution which prescribe that fidelity to the nation and loyalty to the State are fundamental political duties of all citizens. Such duties of fidelity and loyalty, as expressed in the Constitution, do not prohibit or restrict disagreement with the content of the Constitution nor with the actions of government as the criticism of government policy is part of the right to freedom of expression in Art 40.6.1° (i).

---

[22] O Doyle, *Constitutional Law: Text, Cases and Materials* (Clarus Press, Dublin, 2008), p 4.
[23] [2003] 1 IR 1.
[24] [2004] ECR I-9925.
[25] O Doyle, *Constitutional Law: Text, Cases and Materials* (Clarus Press, Dublin, 2008), p 4.
[26] Art 9.2.1°.
[27] *McGimpsey v Ireland* [1990] 1 IR 110, 123.

### 3.2.2 Democracy and Ireland

Article 5 declares Ireland to be a "sovereign, independent, democratic state". Pringle J *obiter* in *de Búrca v Attorney General* discussed the meaning of the State as "democratic" in the following terms:

> "A democracy, as I understand it, is a form of government in which the sovereign power resides in the people as a whole and is exercised by the people either directly or through their elected representatives. This obviously does not mean that every citizen has the right to take part personally in the government of the country."[28]

In the case, the State tried to rely on the former royal prerogative of immunity from suit but it was held to be contrary to the Constitution and had not been carried over to the Irish Free State and therefore into the 1937 constitution.

The provisions are subject to more clarity in the following Article which underpins the democratic nature of the workings of government. Article 6 deals with the source of power of the Irish nation. Even though it mentions the separation of powers[29] theory in the Constitution, where power is broken up between the legislature, executive and judiciary, it places the citizens at the heart of the democratic process. It states that all power is derived, under God, from the people, whose right it is to designate the rulers of the State and, in final appeal, to decide all questions of national policy, according to the requirements of the common good. The right is also qualified in terms of the legitimate exercise of power by stating that they are only exercisable "by or on the authority of the organs of State established by this Constitution".

This provision was tested in *Byrne v Ireland*,[30] in which the plaintiff sought to sue the State for personal injuries caused by roadworks carried out by State employees. In the High Court, Murnaghan J ruled that the sovereignty of the State from the provisions of Art 5 did not allow for the State to be sued in its own courts. However, on appeal to the Supreme Court, Walsh J stated that the State was subject to the Constitution and therefore subject to the people and accordingly, as the courts had a constitutional duty to enforce the Constitution, the plaintiff could assert her rights against the State through the judiciary.[31]

---

[28] [1976] IR 38.
[29] See section 5.1 for a complete consideration of the separation of powers in relation to the organs of government.
[30] [1972] IR 241.
[31] O Doyle, *Constitutional Law: Text, Cases and Materials* (Clarus Press, Dublin, 2008), p 4.

The constitutional interpretation of the role of the citizen as envisaged in Art 6.1 has rested between the realms of political theory and secondary judicial argument. Pursuant to *McKenna v An Taoiseach (No.2)*,[32] *Coughlan v Broadcasting Complaints Commission*[33] and *Doherty v Referendum Commission*,[34] the recent consideration of the role has been interpreted as a postscript to solidify the boundaries of the organs of government regarding referendum communications. However, the constitutional phrasing pursuant to Art 6.1 has clearly placed the citizen at the heart of policy debates.

The original consideration of the citizen and their role in Irish democracy was to arise in the case *Crotty v An Taoiseach*.[35] In the High Court, Barrington J tried to balance the constitutional provisions relating to the State in Art 1, the role of the citizen in Art 6.1 and the role of the legislature in Art 15 along with international relations pursuant to Art 29.4.1°. The learned judge stated that these combined provisions represented the general framework of the institutions pursuant to Art 5 of the Constitution.[36] On the "final appeal" aspect, Barrington J held that the Constitution only laid down three methods: general elections under Art 16, Art 27 referral and general referendum to amend the provisions of the Constitution,[37] adding that "no citizen has a constitutional right to obtain a referendum".[38] In the Supreme Court, the issue of Art 6.1 and the role of the citizen were raised by Walsh J, referencing Budd J in *Boland v An Taoiseach*,[39] who stated the "essential nature of sovereignty is the right to say yes or to say no".[40]

The ability to say yes or no in a manner of responsibly carrying out a citizen's role of final arbiter is predicated on the ability to access and discuss relevant information. Regarding the issue at hand and the implementation of Art 6.1, Walsh J stated that treaty changes contemplated fettered the power of the State to act in international affairs and therefore required "recourse to the people" as they are the guardians of the Constitution.[41] Henchy J also cited Art 6.1 as a means for preventing the prospective government action stating that:

---

[32] [1995] 2 IR 10.

[33] [2000] 3 IR 1.

[34] [2012] IEHC 211.

[35] [1987] IR 713.

[36] "... sovereign, independent, democratic state." [1987] IR 713 at 727.

[37] [1987] IR 713, 745.

[38] *ibid* at 745. This position is accepted, as there are no direct democracy provisions in the Irish Constitution, even if they have been referred to in subsequent judgments.

[39] [1974] IR 338 at 366.

[40] [1987] IR 713 at 745.

[41] *ibid* at 783–784.

> "It follows that the common good of the Irish people is the ultimate standard by which the constitutional validity of the conduct of foreign affairs by the Government is to be judge. In this and in a number of other respects throughout the Constitution the central position of the common good of the Irish people is stressed as one of the most fundamental characteristics of Ireland as a sovereign, independent, democratic state."[42]

In the determination of such issue and seeking relief for fundamental rights, Murray J in *Sinnott v Minister for Education* stated that "the obligation to ensure that the constitutional duty of the State is fulfilled lies in the first instance with the relevant organs of government referred to in Article 6 of the Constitution".[43] In the same case, Denham J that the Constitution is

> "a constitution of the people expressing principles for its society. It sets the norms for the community. It is a document for the people of Ireland, not an economy or a commercial company".[44]

The nature of the role was further expanded in *Re Article 26 and the Electoral Amendment Bill 1983*.[45] In this case, the provisions of the Electoral Amendment Bill to extend the franchise for Dáil elections to British citizens pursuant to the British Nationality Act 1981 that are ordinarily resident in a constituency and over the age of 18. O'Higgins CJ stated:

> "There can be little doubt that 'the people' here referred to are the people of Ireland by, and for, whom the Constitution was enacted. In short, this Article proclaims that it is the Irish people who are the rulers of Ireland and that from them, under God, all power of government derive and that by them the rulers are designated and national policy decided."[46]

The Supreme Court decided that the Bill was unconstitutional due to the interpretation of the word 'people'[47] "from whom all powers derive and who have the right to decide all questions of national policy". Therefore, only citizens can elect members to the Dáil under

---

42  *ibid* at 787.
43  [2001] 2 IR 545 at 682.
44  *ibid* at 664.
45  [1984] IR 268.
46  [1984] IR 268 at 275.
47  *ibid* at 275–276.

Art 16 and expanding the franchise in the manner envisaged by the Bill would be unconstitutional. To allow for British citizens to vote it was necessary to amend the constitution and the provision was approved by the people as the 9th Amendment to the Constitution Act 1984.

In *Russell v Fanning*,[48] the issue of the ability of citizens to decide national policy under Art 6.1 was raised in a case regarding extradition warrants issued for the plaintiff. The warrants related to his delivery to Northern Ireland to serve 20 years imprisonment for criminal offences carried out while a member of the IRA. The plaintiff claimed that the offences were political, regarding questions of national policy, and therefore immune from the provisions of s 50 of the Extradition Act 1965. Finlay CJ summed up the policy argument using Art 6.1. as follows[49]:

> "The Constitution and in particular Article 6, ss.1 and 2 make it clear that, subject to the provisions of the Constitution, decisions as to the method by which the national territory is to be re-integrated are matter for the Government subject to the control of Dáil Éireann, and that the carrying out of those decisions is exercisable only by or on the authority of the organs of State established by the Constitution. Any person or group of persons is, of course, entitled to advocate a particular policy of re-integration, whether that is or is not consistent with existing government policy from time to time. For a person or group of persons, however, to take over or seek to take over the carrying out of the policy of re-integration decided upon himself or themselves without the authority of the organs of State established by the Constitution is to subvert the constitution and usurp the functions of government."[50]

---

[48]  [1988] IR 505.

[49]  Hogan and Whyte consider this reference to be problematic—they cite Art 29.5.2° which states that the Dáil can only control the government in the ratification of international instruments where public funds are at issue and the power to incorporate international instruments is gifted to the Oireachtas as opposed to the Dáil under the provisions of Art 29.6. G Hogan and G Whyte, *JM Kelly: The Irish Constitution* (4th ed, Tottel Publishing, Dublin 2006), p 106. Furthermore, the precedent of *Crotty v An Taoiseach* [1987] IR 713 may also be cited as further weight against this idea, as the judgment was clear on the parameters of international agreements and the power of the State on this issue. Also, see the 19th Amendment of the Constitution Act 1998 which revised the historically problematic issue of Arts 2 and 3 of the Constitution as part of the Good Friday Agreement which changed the boundaries of the State and the mechanism for any possible re-integration.

[50]  [1988] IR 505 at 530.

Hederman J stated that the provisions of Art 6.1 should be considered as follows:

> "Article 6 of the Constitution is the article which sets out the divisions of powers of government between the executive, the legislature and the judiciary and declares that all power of the government derive 'under God, from the People, whose right it is to designate the rulers of the State and, in final appeal, to divide all questions of national policy, according to the requirements of the common good.' It goes on to provide that 'these powers of government are exercisable only by or on the authority of the organs of State established by this Constitution'."[51]

## 3.3 Ireland and International Law

Article 29 outlines the relationship between the Irish State and both other countries and special regimes in the context of public international law as follows:

> "Article 29
>
> 1 Ireland affirms its devotion to the ideal of peace and friendly co-operation amongst nations founded on international justice and morality.
>
> 2 Ireland affirms its adherence to the principle of the pacific settlement of international disputes by international arbitration or judicial determination.
>
> 3 Ireland accepts the generally recognised principles of international law as its rule of conduct in its relations with other States.
>
> 4 1° The executive power of the State in or in connection with its external relations shall in accordance with Article 28 of this Constitution be exercised by or on the authority of the Government."

In Art 29.1, the Constitution affirms the nation's devotion to the "ideal of peace and friendly co-operation amongst nations founded on international justice and morality". It also "affirms its adherence to the principle of the pacific settlement of international disputes by international arbitration or judicial determination". In Art 29.3, the

---

[51]  *ibid* at 537.

State accepts the principles of public international law in relation to its conduct with other States. This would include both the League of Nations and the United Nations, as the Constitution has spanned both international organisations. Only the government may exercise the executive power of the State in relation to its external relations. This creates what is known as a dualist State with regard to international relations, in that any treaties which are signed by Ireland only affect Ireland in terms of their international relations with other States but have no bearing on the domestic jurisdiction. It is for this reason that we need referendums to pass international treaties into domestic law, such as the treaty dealing with the international criminal court. It is also the reason why many UN Declarations have no bearing on Irish human rights law.

Article 29.2 sets out the dualist nature of Irish international relations which allows for the government to adopt any organ, instrument, or method by the members of any group or league of nations with which the State is or becomes associated for the purpose of international co-operation in matters of common concern. This means in practice that the Irish government is free to sign any international treaties or declarations, but they do not become justiciable in the Irish jurisdiction until they become part of Irish law. An example of this would be the European Convention on Human Rights. Ireland was a signatory of the document from its foundation but the rights enshrined in the convention could only be used in an Irish court when it became part of Irish law through the European Convention on Human Rights Act 2003. The impact of this can be seen in the *Norris v Ireland*[52] case, where provisions of the Offences against the Person Act 1861 and the Criminal Law Amendment Act 1885 criminalised homosexual activities and were found to be incompatible with Art 8 of the Convention. Even though this was a clear statement that Irish law on this matter was contrary to human rights, this judgment had no impact on the operation of the criminal law in Ireland. The issue was finally resolved when the Criminal Justice (Sexual Offences) Act 1993 decriminalised these activities in Ireland. Article 29.2 also references the many international bodies which the State has entered into such as the European Atomic Energy Community[53] and the International Criminal Court.[54]

Under the provisions of Art 29.5.1°, every international agreement to which the State becomes a party must be laid before the Dáil. The State will not be bound by an international agreement which will result in

---

[52]  (1991) 13 EHRR 186.
[53]  Art 29.3.
[54]  Art 29.9.

the State being financially liable. It will not be effective unless the Dáil has approved of the agreement.[55] This does not include agreements or conventions of a technical or administrative nature.[56]

Article 29.8 allows for the State to exercise "extra-territorial jurisdiction in accordance with the generally recognised principles of international law". This allows for the State to extend its jurisdiction outside of the boundaries of the State, as stated in Art 3 of the constitution.

## 3.4 Ireland and Membership of the EU

The many referendums dealing with the EU and its treaties are due to the case of *Crotty v An Taoiseach*.[57] Here the plaintiff successfully stopped the government from ratifying the Single European Act as it was incompatible with the Constitution and therefore needed the assent of the citizens in order for it to be ratified. The remainder of this Article details the EU treaties which the State has ratified through referendums. The procedure for ratifying treaties is also set out in the Article. Even though the international relations Article clearly states that external relations is a reserved power of the executive, as formulated by Walsh J "the Government is the sole organ of the State in the field of international relations".[58] The essence of the jurisprudence on the issue is encapsulated in the following excerpt from Walsh J as follows:

> "In enacting the Constitution the people conferred full freedom of action upon the Government to decide matters of foreign policy and to act as it thinks fit on any particular issue so far as policy is concerned and as, in the opinion of the Government, the occasion requires. In my view, this freedom does not carry with it the power to abdicate that freedom or to enter into binding agreements with other States to exercise that power in a particular way or to refrain from exercising it save by particular procedures, and so to bind the State in its freedom of action in its foreign policy. The freedom to formulate foreign policy is just as much a mark of sovereignty as the freedom to form economic policy and the freedom to legislate. The latter two have now been curtailed by the consent of the people to the amendment of the Constitution which is contained in Article 29, s. 4, sub-s. 3 of the Constitution. If it is now

---

[55] Art 29.5.2°.
[56] Art 29.5.3°.
[57] [1987] IR 713.
[58] *ibid* at 782.

desired to qualify, curtail or inhibit the existing sovereign power to formulate and to pursue such foreign policies as from time to time to the Government may seem proper, it is not within the power of the Government itself to do so. The foreign policy organ of the State cannot, within the terms of the Constitution, agree to impose upon itself, the State or upon the people the contemplated restrictions upon freedom of action. To acquire the power to do so would, in my opinion, require a recourse to the people "whose right it is" in the words of Article 6 ". . . in final appeal, to decide all questions of national policy, according to the requirements of the common good." In the last analysis it is the people themselves who are the guardians of the Constitution. In my view, the assent of the people is a necessary prerequisite to the ratification of so much of the Single European Act".[59]

The result of the judgment is that all treaties which have obligations contained in them where there are "binding agreements with other States to exercise that power in a particular way or to refrain from exercising it save by particular procedures, and so to bind the State in its freedom of action in its foreign policy", they must be subject to referendum. Therefore, any treaty which binds the State in this manner, such as the treaty requirements dealing with the International Criminal Court to subsequent European treaties must be put before the people in a referendum.

Under Art 29.4, the State "affirms its commitment to the EU within which the member States of that Union work together to promote peace, shared values and the well-being of their peoples".

Over the course of Ireland's membership of the EU and with the impact of the *Crotty* judgment, any treaties which the State must be a signatory of must be passed by referendum. For example, the ratification of the Lisbon Treaty is found in Art 29.5.[60] Protocols which the State may exercise options or discretions on, such as the Schengen Agreement, are dealt with in Art 29.7.1(ii). Schengen refers to the open borders approach of many EU countries which allows for people to move freely within Europe. Ireland and the UK did not follow this approach, though the Houses of the Oireachtas are granted the power to approve of this measure. Article 29.8 allows for the State to agree to decisions, regulations or other acts from the Council of the European Union and legislation but any decision, regulation or act relating to

---

[59] [1987] IR 713 at 783–784.
[60] This treaty was originally rejected by the people, but was eventually passed as the 28th Amendment of the Constitution.

freedom, security and justice shall be subject to the prior approval of both Houses of the Oireachtas. Article 29.9 removes Ireland from any common defence policy. Article 29.10 was inserted by referendum to allow for the State to ratify the Treaty on Stability, Coordination and Governance in the Economic and Monetary Union. There is also a planned referendum to be held on Ireland's proposed membership of the European Patent Court.

# THE PRESIDENT

## 4.0 Introduction

The Office of President was established under the 1937 Constitution. Prior to this, the equivalent office was held by the Governor General. The effect of creating the Office of President effectively supplanted the role and responsibility of the Governor General and created a Head of State for a fully independent Ireland.[1] There have been eight Presidents to date, with the current President being Michael D Higgins.

The President plays an important role in all the organs of government. The President signs legislation into law.[2] The President appoints the Taoiseach[3] and the other members of the executive.[4] The President also appoints judges under the provisions of the Constitution.[5] Therefore it is essential to examine the role, responsibilities and constitutional activities of the President along with the organs of government. The divisions of these branches of government is central to the separation of powers.[6]

## 4.1 Powers of the President

The provisions for the President are set out in Art 12. The President is formally known as Uachtarán na hÉireann and takes precedence over all other persons in the State. Article 12.2.1° states that the President is to be elected by direct vote of the people. Every citizen with a right to vote at Dáil Elections has a right to vote for the President.[7] The voting is conducted by secret ballot and by means of proportional representation by the single transferable vote. The election must take place no later than 60 days after the previous President has left office. Every citizen over the age of 35 is entitled to run for election to the office.[8] Everyone seeking election, unless they were a former or retiring President, must be nominated by either 20 Oireachtas members or not less than four councils. Each nominating body or Oireachtas member can only nominate one candidate. When only one candidate is nominated, there is no need for an election. The term of office for

---

[1] See chapter 2 dealing with the history of the Constitution for details of the dilution and ultimate removal of the Governor General and British rule in Ireland.

[2] Art 13.3.1°.

[3] Art 13.1.1°.

[4] Art 13.1.2°.

[5] Art 35.1.

[6] The theory of the separation of powers will be considered in section 5.1.

[7] For a further discussion of the electoral process, see section 5.2.7.

[8] It was proposed to reduce the age for eligibility to run for office to 21 in the 35th Amendment of the Constitution (Age of Eligibility for Election to the Office of President) Bill 2015 but this was defeated by referendum on the same day as the successful marriage equality referendum.

the President is seven years from the date when they enter office.[9] It is possible for an elected President to seek re-election to office but they may only be re-elected for a single term.[10] Former or retiring Presidents may nominate themselves.[11]

The President cannot be a member of the Oireachtas, and if he was one prior to election, then he must vacate his seat. The President cannot hold any other office or salaried position. Article 12.8 sets down the oath of office which must be taken in the presence of members of both Houses of the Oireachtas, and judges of the Supreme Court and the High Court as follows:

> "In the presence of Almighty God I do solemnly and sincerely promise and declare that I will maintain the Constitution of Ireland and uphold its laws, that I will fulfil my duties faithfully and conscientiously in accordance with the Constitution and the law, and that I will dedicate my abilities to the service and welfare of the people of Ireland. May God direct and sustain me."

The President cannot leave the State during his term of office except with the consent of the government. The President may be impeached by the members of the Oireachtas for stated misbehaviour. However, the motion to impeach must be supported by over 30 members of the House and the overall vote must be supported by a two-thirds majority. Where one House has made the charge, the other House must either investigate or commission the investigation of the charge. The President has a right to appear and be represented at such investigations. If on the basis of these investigations there is a resolution passed by two-thirds of the total members of the Houses of the Oireachtas, the then President will be deemed to be unfit for office and will be removed. Article 12.11.1° states that the President will have an official residence in or near the City of Dublin. This residence is known as Áras an Úachtarain and is located in Phoenix Park in Dublin. The President can be paid and the amounts cannot be reduced during the President's term in office.

The Office of the President is interconnected with all the organs of government. The President appoints the Taoiseach, the Ministers, and the judiciary, and he also acts in the dissolution of parliament.

---

[9] Art 12.3.1°.
[10] Art 12.3.2°. Sean T O'Kelly, Eamonn de Valera and Patrick Hillary served the full two terms of office. They did not face re-election for the second term as they were each the only candidate.
[11] Mary Robinson is the only previous President that can nominate herself as she is the only former President that did not serve two terms.

Therefore, under the Irish construction of the separation of powers,[12] the President is at the heart of government. On consideration of the central role of the President, it is arguable that for this reason, there are relatively few powers given to the President to exercise independently without reference to either the Council of State or cabinet.

## 4.2 Presidential Commission

In the case of the President being unable to perform his duties or in his absence, the Presidential Commission is capable of exercising the powers of the President. There is no Vice-Presidential role in the Irish Constitution. For example, when President Erskine Childers passed away in office, the Presidential Commission was able to act until the new President took office. The new President was Cearbhall Ó Dálaigh, who later resigned, so again, the Commission had to step in to act.

Article 14 deals with the Presidential Commission which will act during the absence of the President, temporary or permanent incapacity. There is no vice-presidential role in the Irish Constitution. The Commission will also act in the event of the death, resignation, removal from office, or failure to exercise and perform the powers and functions of his office or any of them, or at any time at which the office of President may be vacant. The Commission consists of the Chief Justice, the Chairman of Dáil Éireann (An Ceann Comhairle), and the Chairman of Seanad Éireann. The President of the High Court may also act as a member of the Commission when the Chief Justice is unavailable. The Deputy Chair of the Dáil may also act in place of the Ceann Comhairle when the Ceann Comhairle is unavailable; likewise with the Deputy Chair of the Seanad.For example, when President Erskine Childers passed away in office, the Presidential Commission was able to act until the new President took office. The new President was Cearbhall Ó Dálaigh who later resigned, so again, the Commission had to step in to act.

## 4.3 The Council of State

The majority of the powers of the President require the President to consult with the Council of State. The purpose of the Council of State is to aid and counsel the President on the exercise of his power. The Council of State is made up of the Taoiseach, the Tánaiste, the Chief Justice, the President of the High Court, the Chairman of Dáil Éireann, the Chairman of Seanad Éireann, and the Attorney General as ex officio members. It is also made up of

---

[12] See full discussion on the theory and interpretation of the separation of powers in the next chapter at section 5.1.

"Every person able and willing to act as a member of the Council of State who shall have held the Office of President, or the office of Taoiseach, or the office of Chief Justice, or the Office of President of the Executive Council of Saorstát Éireann"[13]

The president is entitled to appoint others to the Council, but no more than seven.

Every member of the Council is to subscribe to the following declaration after their first meeting under the provisions of Art 31.4:

"In the presence of Almighty God I do solemnly and sincerely promise and declare that I will faithfully and conscientiously fulfil my duties as a member of the Council of State."

Every member of the Council of State appointed by the President will hold Office until the successor for the President is appointed. Members of the Council are entitled to resign by placing their resignation into the hands of the President. The President is also entitled to terminate the appointment of any member appointed by him. Meetings of the Council will be scheduled when and where the President requires them. Under the provisions of Art 32, the President cannot perform or exercise the constitutional duties which require the convening of the Council of State unless the members of the Council have been heard by the President. This does not mean that the President must do what is suggested by the Council, but that the President has been briefed before deciding on a course of action.

Under Art 13.3, the President may at any time, after consultation with the Council of State, convene a meeting of either or both of the Houses of the Oireachtas. Furthermore, under the provisions of Art 13.7.1° the President, after consulting with the Council of State, may communicate with Houses of the Oireachtas in regard to any matter of national or public importance. After consulting with the Council of State, the President may also send a message to the nation on any matter. However, such public addresses must receive the approval of the government.

## 4.4 President and Relationship with Government

As the President's powers transcend the division of governmental

---

[13] Art 31.2.ii.

power under the separation of powers doctrine, it is essential that the role and powers of the President are clearly set out in the Constitution. Of all the constitutional offices set out in the Constitution, the Office of President is the most detailed.

Article 13 sets out the relationship between the President and the government. Article 13.1 states that the President shall, on the nomination of the Dáil, appoint the Taoiseach and the other members of the government under Art 13.2. The President can also, on the advice of the Taoiseach accept the resignation or terminate the appointment of any Minister. The Dáil will be summoned and dissolved by the President on the advice of the Taoiseach. However, the President at his discretion may refuse to dissolve the Dáil where the Taoiseach has lost support of a majority of the Dáil.

Under the provisions of Art 13.4, supreme command of the Defence Forces is vested in the President, but the exercise of this power will be regulated by law. All commissioned officers in the Defence Forces hold their commission from the President. The President also has the power to pardon, commute and reduce the punishment of any person imprisoned in Ireland by a criminal court. However, this power is also vested by law in other bodies.

Article 13.8.1° states that the President is not answerable to either House in the performance of his duties. Since most of the actions that may be taken by the President are done in consultation with either the government or the Council of State, nearly all duties are done in accordance with their counsel. However, if there is a question over the activities of the President, even in spite of such constitutional constraints, any questionable behaviour may be reviewed under the impeachment process as detailed in the Constitution, and such behaviour may be reviewed under Art 12.10 for investigation.

The vast majority of the powers and functions that are conferred on the President in the Constitution are only to be used where the advice of government has been sought or acts with consultation with the Council of State under Art 13.9. There are only a few instances where the President has discretion to act alone, such as in dissolving the Dáil under Art 13.2.2° or the appointment of members of the Council of State under Art 31.3. Additional functions may be prescribed to the President by law. The main Article dealing with the President concludes with stating that no power or function vested in the President may be exercised without consultation with the government. In reality, it could be argued that the President is merely a figurehead for the State and is under the guidance of either government or the

Council of State in the exercise of his or her powers, except when it comes to a limited range of activities such as selecting nominees to the Council of State, the final decisions on whether to bring Art 26 and Art 27 challenges and convening a meeting of the joint Houses.

## 4.5 Legislation and the President

Under the provisions of Art 13.3.1°, every Bill which is passed or deemed to be passed by both Houses of the Oireachtas must be sent to the President for signature.[14] The President is under a duty to promulgate every law that is made by the Oireachtas, unless the provisions of either Art 26 or Art 27 are triggered by the President. As part of the President's duty to uphold the constitution, with regard to the legislative process, the President may use either article to protect the constitution and the rights contained therein. These methods allow for the constitutionality of legislation to be tested through an Art 26 referral or for the will of the people to be assessed on legislation though an Art 27 ordinary referendum.

Under the provisions of Art 26, the President may send legislation to the Supreme Court to test its constitutionality. This option is open to all legislation bar Money Bills, Constitutional Amendment Bills or an Abridged Time Bill. In order to trigger this procedure, the President must consult with the Council of State and then send the Bill to the Supreme Court to test its constitutionality. This procedure must take place within seven days of the Bill being sent to the President by the Taoiseach for signature. While the process is underway, the President is not allowed to sign the Bill into law.

When hearing the application, at least five members of the Supreme Court will consider the question that is sent to it. The Attorney General will represent the government's side and counsel will be assigned to represent the other side of the question. The Supreme Court will pronounce its decision no later than 60 days after the reference. Where the Supreme Court holds that the legislation in question is unconstitutional, then the President cannot sign it into law. This is true even when only a portion of the Bill offends against the Constitution, as the Supreme Court will not exclude the unconstitutional elements. The entire Bill is rejected. However, one of the major drawbacks of the procedure is the fact that legislation which survives an Art 26 challenge cannot be judicially reviewed in the future. This is due to Arts 26.2

---

[14] Bills are deemed to be passed where the Seanad has rejected legislation. The Seanad does not have a veto on legislation but is able to delay legislation by 180 days. When this time period has elapsed, the Bill is deemed to have been passed by the Seanad and sent for signature to the President.

and 34.3[15] which do not allow for any other opinion to be pronounced on the legislation. This interpretation was upheld in the case of *Re Ó Láighléis*,[16] where it was held that irrespective of the merits of the case, the constitutionality of the Offences against the State (Amendment) Act 1940 had been upheld in an Art 26 challenge.

Under Art 27, any Bill, bar a proposal to amend the Constitution, can be sent to the people in a referendum. In order to trigger this process, under the provisions of Art 27.1, a majority of the Seanad and not less than one-third of the Dáil in a joint petition addressed to the President requesting that he decline to sign the legislation, as it contains a proposal of such national importance that the people should express their views by means of a vote. The statement should contain the reasons or grounds upon which this request is made and should be presented to the President not later than four days after the Bill has been deemed to be passed by both Houses.

When the President receives such a request under the Article, he must consult with the Council of State and must give his decision within 10 days of the Bill passing or being deemed to pass both Houses. If the legislation in question has already been considered to be constitutional by the Supreme Court under the provisions of Art 26, it may still be sent to the people. If the President decides to accept the Art 27 petition, then the Taoiseach and the Chair of each House must be informed in writing. The President then has two options: either to send the Bill to the people in order to veto the legislation under the provisions of Art 47 within 18 months, or to see a resolution of the Dáil to dissolve and re-assemble; i.e. base a general election on the will of the people over the legislation at issue.

When the will of the people has been determined and the Bill is passed, the President will sign the legislation into law. If the Art 27 petition is not accepted by the President, then again the Taoiseach and the Chair of each House must be informed in writing and the Bill will be signed within 11 days after being deemed to be passed by both Houses.

---

[15] See the section on the courts and the trial of offences in the next chapter.
[16] [1960] IR 93.

# CHAPTER FIVE

# GOVERNMENT AND THE CONSTITUTION

## 5.0 Introduction

The powers of government are split between the organs of State: the legislature, the executive and the judiciary as per Art 6.1.[1] For the purposes of this book, this chapter will look at the concept of the separation of powers in general and will then focus on the legislature and the executive. The courts will be considered in the next chapter.

The reason for splitting the powers of government between three branches is to prevent the concentration of power in one body without means of checks and balances from other organs. This theory, known as the separation of powers, is detailed below. This section will analyse the theoretical interpretation of the doctrine and its application in the Irish constitutional framework in relation to the legislature and the executive. The electoral system will be looked at in this chapter. This chapter will also consider the position of local government in the Constitution and the constitutional powers of the Attorney General and the Comptroller and Auditor General.

## 5.1 The Separation of Powers

The provisions of Art 6 allow for the implementation of division within the organs of government. The organs of government are taken to mean the legislature, the executive and the judiciary. In the Irish context, the legislature is the Oireachtas, as they create the laws which govern the State. The executive is taken to mean the cabinet or Government where the Ministers, Taoiseach and Tánaiste exercise their power. The judiciary is the courts. All of these organs take their power and degree of responsibility from the Constitution. The legislature finds its power in Art 15.2.1°, the executive takes their power from Art 28.2 and the courts take theirs from Art 34.1.

The concept of the separation of powers predates the Constitution or the State and it is found in many other constitutions, such as the Constitution of the United States and the French Constitution. In general, separation of powers is the idea that the organs of government are equal in power to each other and one cannot direct the other organs as to a proposed course of action. In practice, however, there are difficulties with a strict adherence to this theory in Ireland. For example, the legislature is controlled by the majority parties in the Dáil. The members of the legislature can also be members of the cabinet which is the executive. There is therefore a very strong connection between the executive and the legislature, and on a day to day basis, the

---

[1]  See section 3.2.1.2.

will of the executive directs the legislature. Furthermore, the judiciary is appointed by the President, who is a member of the executive, and the nominations are on instructions of government.

In *Buckley (Sinn Féin) v Attorney General*[2] the oft-cited formulation of the doctrine of the separation of power for the Irish constitutional context is stated as

> "The manifest object of [Article 6] was to recognise and ordain that, in the State, all powers of government should be exercised in accordance with the well-recognised principle of the distribution of powers between the legislative, executive and judicial organs of the State and to require that these powers should not be exercised otherwise. The subsequent articles are designed to carry into effect this distribution of powers."[3]

In the judgment of Ó Dálaigh CJ in *Re Haughey*,[4] the tripartite separation of powers stated in *Buckley* was reaffirmed.[5] *Boland v An Taoiseach*[6] concerned the interpretation of the international relations article of the Constitution and the power of the government to sign such agreements without recourse to the citizens by way of referendum. The particular agreement in question in this case was the Sunningdale Agreement. In the Supreme Court, Fitzgerald CJ stated that Art 6 of the Constitution established

> "... beyond question the separation of the executive, legislative and judicial powers of government ... Consequently, in my opinion, the courts have no power, either express or implied, to supervise or interfere with the exercise by the Government of its executive functions, unless the circumstances are such as to amount to a clear disregard by the Government of the powers and duties conferred upon it by the Constitution."[7]

---

2    *Buckley and Others (Sinn Féin) v Attorney General* [1950] IR 67.
3    [1950] IR 67 at 81.
4    *In Re Haughey* [1971] IR 217.
5    "The Constitution of Ireland is founded on the doctrine of the tripartite division of the powers of government—legislative, executive and judicial—as appears from an examination of Articles 6, 15, 28 and 34" [1971] IR 217 at 250.
6    [1974] IR 338, and Budd J at 366 where the role of the judiciary in policy matters was considered stating that the "Government is responsible to the Dáil which can support or oppose those policies and review them.' Also see Griffin J at 369 which restated the principle laid down in *Buckley and Others (Sinn Féin) v Attorney General* [1950] IR 67 at 81 as discussed above.
7    [1974] IR 338 at 361–362. This section was also cited with approval by Denham J in *Sinnott v Minister for Education* [2001] 2 IR 545 at 659.

The case of *Sinnott v Attorney General*,[8] the focus of debate and analysis in the judgment rested on the right to education with the consideration of the separation of powers as an ancillary, yet fundamental, issue to be decided. Referring to this tripartite division of powers, Hardiman J stated that such decisions are not just for "demarcation or administrative convenience" but the "constitutional arrangements of all free societies"'.[9]

> "In my view, conflicts of priorities, values, modes of administration or sentiments cannot be avoided or ignored by adopting an agreed or imposed exclusive theory of justice. And if judges were to become involved in such an enterprise, designing the details of policy in individual cases or in general, and ranking some areas of policy in priority to others, they would step beyond their appointed role. The views of aspirants to judicial office on such social and economic questions are not canvassed for the good reason that they are thought to be irrelevant. They have no mandate in these areas. And the legislature and the executive, possessed of a democratic mandate, are liable to recall by the withdrawal of that mandate. That is the most fundamental, but by no means the only, basis of the absolute necessity for judicial restraint in these areas. To abandon this restraint would be unacceptably and I believe unconstitutionally to limit the proper freedom of action of the legislature and the executive branch of government."[10]

In the judgment of Denham J, the separation of powers was discussed as follows

> "All powers of government derive from the people: Article 6.1. These powers are exercised by the organs of government established by the Constitution, being legislative, executive and judicial. The functions of government are divided between these three branches of government ... In addition to recognising and applying the doctrine of the separation of powers it is important to afford respect to the decisions of each of the constitutional organs of State. It is from this basis that analysis of governmental decisions commences. ... However, I would not exclude the rare and exceptional case, where, to protect constitutional rights, the court may

---

[8]   [2001] 2 IR 545.
[9]   *ibid* at 699.
[10]  *ibid* at 711.

have a jurisdiction and even a duty to make a mandatory order."[11]

Denham J went on to cite[12] the judgments in both *Crotty v An Taoiseach*,[13] which laid down the activities and boundaries of the State and *Murphy v Dublin Corporation*, where Walsh J stated that no one of the three organs is given a paramount place

> "As the legislative, executive, and judicial powers are all exercised under and on behalf of the State, the interest of State, as such, is always involved. The division of powers does give paramountcy in all circumstances to any one of the organs exercising the powers of government over the other."[14]

The case of *T.D. v Minister for Education*[15] also referred to a citizen seeking the vindication of the personal rights against the Oireachtas. The vindication of such rights was also based on the tenuous balance of the separation of powers. In dealing with the separation of powers aspect, Keane CJ relied on previous cases[16] stating that

> "Both the High Court and this court have stressed on more than one occasion that, where the Oireachtas or the executive are found, whether by act or omission, to have acted in a manner which violates the Constitution, they are entitled to expect that the other responsible arms of Government will take such steps as are necessary to redress the wrongs in question."[17]

Regarding the rationale for the use of separation of powers relating to the role of the Oireachtas and the executive in the determination of matters of policy and the distribution of funds, it was said that:

> "The difficulty created by the order of the High Court in this case is not simply that it offends in principle against the doctrine of the separation of powers, ... It also involves the High Court in effectively determining the policy which the Executive are to follow ... i.e., an adjudication on the

---

[11] [2001] 2 IR 545 at 635.
[12] *ibid* at 655–656.
[13] Finlay CJ in *Crotty v An Taoiseach* [1987] IR 713, 772.
[14] [1972] IR 215 at 234.
[15] *T.D. v Minister for Education* [2001] 4 IR 259.
[16] Specifically *Buckley and Others (Sinn Féin) v Attorney General* [1950] IR 67, *Boland v An Taoiseach* [1974] IR 338 as discussed in this section.
[17] [2001] 4 IR 259 at 286.

fairness or otherwise of the manner in which other organs of State had administered public resources. ... [S]ince the High Court first began the difficult task of grappling with this problem, a Rubicon has been crossed, clearly with the best of motives, in which it is moving to undertake a role which is conferred by the Constitution on the other organs of State, who are also entrusted with the resources necessary to discharge that role in the interests of the common good."[18]

The importance of the separation of powers was also stated succinctly by Denham J in the following excerpt:

"Fundamental powers of government are distributed between these three great organs of State. A separation of powers is described although it is not a strict division or distribution of power. It is not a doctrine applied rigidly in the Constitution. A framework for government is established which includes a functional separation of powers to independent organs of State. It is the separation and independence of the institutions which is important."[19]

Denham J regarded the operation and availability of judicial review and its impact on the operation of democracy as important as it represented a step away from the Westminster model of governance.[20] The judgment of Murray J was based on an assessment of the first principles of the doctrine of the separation of powers, especially the writings of Montesquieu,[21] and he considered the doctrine an "essential and inherent part of the modern liberal democracy founded on the rule

---

[18] *ibid* at 287–288.

[19] *ibid* at 299. See also Denham J in *Laurentiu v Minister for Justice* [1994] 4 IR 26 where similar sentiments are expressed at 60.

[20] "It was a sophisticated step taken by the people in 1937, to incorporate such a system of judicial review. Previously Ireland had been governed by the Westminster model—the simple parliamentary sovereignty–democratic majority system—where parliament was supreme and the courts did not have such power of constitutional judicial review." Denham J, [2001] 4 IR 259 at 312; see also section 8.3.

[21] [2001] 4 IR 259 at 329, in particular the following section "When the legislative and executive powers are united in the same person or body, there can be no liberty, because apprehensions may arise less the same monarch or senate should enact tyrannical laws to execute them in a tyrannical manner". He expressed the concern: "Were the power of judging joined with the legislative, the life and liberty of the subject would be exposed to arbitrary control, for the judge would then be the legislator. Were it joined to the executive power, the judge might behave with all the violence of an oppressor." See also D. Gwynn Morgan, *The Separation of Powers in the Irish Constitution* (Round Hall Sweet and Maxwell, Dublin, 1997), pp 2–7 for a discussion on the development of the concept of the doctrine of the separation of powers through history at section 5.2.

of law".[22] Under the terms of the Constitution, Murray J considered the application of the doctrine to flow from the respect of powers from each organ of state and the differentiation between policy matters and core constitutional functions[23]:

> "Adopting a policy or a programme and deciding to implement it is a core function of the Executive. It is not for the courts to decide policy or to implement it. It may determine whether such policy or actions to implement such policy are compatible with the law or the Constitution or fulfil obligations. That is not deciding policy."[24]

The judgment of Hardiman J was the first instance of referencing the people in the chain of power involved in the separation of powers:

> "Under our Constitution, all political power in the State derives from the people. By Article 6, this general power is divided into the three major powers of government, the legislative, the executive and the judicial. These powers are separate and distinct in order to prevent any one power, or the individuals who hold it, from becoming dominant."[25]

In spite of this reference, the position of the people as subservient to the organs of government or supreme to the separation of powers was not resolved. It would follow that if the State is one based on popular sovereignty, then the people would be supreme, their power delegated to the Oireachtas and therefore the people are to be served by the separation of powers. There has not yet been a clear elucidation of this role. The cases of *Sinnott* and *TD* illustrate the need to balance the common good when issues of policy are at play. Moreover, the balance between the citizen and the organs of State has yet to be adjudicated. As in *Sinnott* above, the order which was granted by the High Court was found to be in breach of the doctrine of separation of powers and therefore the court allowed the appeal.

## 5.2 The Oireachtas

The parliament comprises of the Dáil and Seanad. The parliament is known as the Oireachtas. The functions of the Oireachtas are to create legislation, to hold the leaders of the government to account, to pass a budget for national spending and to debate issues of national

---

[22] [2001] 4 IR 259 at 329.
[23] *ibid* at 331.
[24] *ibid* at 333 and echoed by Hardiman J in the same case [2001] 4 IR 259 at 338.
[25] [2001] 4 IR 259 at 338.

importance. There is a detailed process set out for the passage of legislation.[26] The President is also considered to be part of the legislative process. In the Constitution, both Houses of the Oireachtas are given separate treatment initially, then their total parliamentary powers are considered later on.

The Constitution deals with the powers granted to both the Dáil and the Seanad in respect of their remit as the legislative body under the treatment of the organs of government. Under the provisions of Art 15, the principal rules surrounding the Oireachtas are laid out: for example, the national parliament is officially known as the Oireachtas under the provisions of the Constitution and it is constituted of the Dáil and the Seanad. The wording describes the Dáil as the House of Representatives and the Seanad as the Senate, which mirrors the US model of democratic institutions. The place for sitting is set down as Dublin. The provision for making legislation is set down in Art 15.2.1° as being solely vested in the Oireachtas. However, this power can be delegated to other bodies, once they do not transgress their powers or the spirit of the primary legislation enacted by the Oireachtas.[27] The Oireachtas is also vested with the power to create functional or vocational councils in order to represent the social and economic life of the people and will be enacted in law to determine their powers and duties. Under Art 15.7, the Oireachtas is to sit at least once every year. The sittings are to be in public unless there is an assent by a two-thirds majority.

Article 15.4.1° states that the Oireachtas shall not pass any law that contravenes or is "repugnant" to the Constitution.[28] Also, if any law or part of a law is found to be "repugnant", then it shall not be valid. This is the main reason for judicial review where a person is claiming that legislation goes against their Constitutional rights. In such a case, the law is deemed to be unconstitutional and has no legal effect. The Oireachtas is precluded from passing any retrospective legislation or legislation which allows for the death penalty. The right to raise and maintain an army is vested in the Oireachtas and no other army may be raised in the State for any purpose.

Under the provisions of Art 15.10, each House is entitled to make its own rules and standing orders, ensure freedom of debate, protect its official documents and private papers and prevent persons from

---

[26] See section 5.2.3 for primary legislation and section 5.2.3.1 for a consideration of delegated legislation.
[27] See section 5.2.3.
[28] See section 5.2.3 relating to the legislative powers and responsibilities of the Oireachtas.

corrupting its members in carrying out their duties. Under Art 15.12, all official reports and publications are privileged. Under Art 15.13, no member of either House can be arrested while leaving, returning or while in the precincts of Leinster House. Also, no statements made in the House can be the subject of court action. This means that no one can sue a politician for what was said in either House if it harmed their good name. This is known as parliamentary privilege.[29]

All questions will be decided by a majority and the Chair, being the Ceann Comhairle, will have the casting vote. The quorum will be decided by the standing orders. No member can be a member of both the Dáil and the Seanad. Also, under Art 15.15 allowances can be paid to members in respect of travelling and other facilities in connection to their duties as public representatives.

### 5.2.1 Dáil

The Dáil is dealt with in Arts 16 and 17 of the Constitution. Under Art 16.1, every citizen who is over the age of 21 is entitled to run as a candidate for election to the Dáil. Anyone over the age of 18 is entitled to vote and the vote will be conducted by secret ballot with one vote only per person. The constituencies for the Dáil will be determined by law but with no less than one member per each 30000 people. The representative ratio will be kept even as far as practicable between constituencies. These constituencies will be based on the previous census and will be reviewed once every 12 years. However, any changes will take place at the next general elections. Each constituency will return at least three members. Members will be elected on the basis of proportional representation by a single transferable vote.[30]

The method for dissolving the Dáil for a general election is set out in Art 13. The elections for Dáil Éireann must take place not later than 30 days afterwards and should take place on the same day in all Constituencies where practicable. However, the islands vote before the mainland in case of weather delays and postal votes are required to be in before the general election day. The Ceann Comhairle is automatically returned to the Dáil without election. The Dáil will meet within 30 days of the election day. The new Dáil cannot continue for more than seven years. Bye-elections are regulated by the Electoral Acts.

---

[29] See section 5.2.6 relating to parliamentary privilege.
[30] See section 5.2.7 dealing with the electoral process.

### 5.2.2 Seanad

The Seanad is covered in Arts 18 and 19 of the Constitution. The Seanad is composed of 60 members. Eleven are nominated by the Taoiseach and the remaining 49 are to be elected. Eligibility for the Seanad is the same as for the Dáil. The elections for the Seanad take place after the completion of the Dáil elections, so it is in the incoming Taoiseach who chooses his nominees to the Seanad. Of the elected members, three will be elected by the NUI constituent Universities[31] and three will be elected from Trinity.

The 7th Amendment of the Constitution in 1979 allowed for the State to extend the University franchise to graduates of other Higher Educational bodies such as the Institutes of Technology, the University of Limerick and Dublin City University. This is reflected in the provisions of Art 18.2(ii) which allows for other institutions of higher education in the State to elect Seanad members to the University Panel. The required legislative amendments to the Electoral Acts to reflect the amendment has not been drafted.

The other members will be elected from panels where they have knowledge and practical experience in the following areas: national language, culture, literature, art and education, agriculture and fisheries, labour, industry and commerce, and public administration. The members elected to each panel will comprise a mix of candidates that are nominated by members of the Oireachtas and candidates that are nominated by the bodies which have the authority to nominate candidates. For example, the Irish Congress of Trade Unions may nominate candidates for election to the Labour Panel of the Seanad.[32] All other issues related to the conduct of Seanad elections will be set by law. Vacancies arising during the term of the Seanad will be filled by either appointment by the Taoiseach to replace one of his nominees, or election, if the vacancy arises from any other member of the Seanad.

### 5.2.3 Legislative Process

Under Art 15.2.1° of Bunreacht ná hÉireann, the Oireachtas is vested with legislative authority. The Article states that "The sole and exclusive power of making laws for the State is hereby vested in the Oireachtas; no other legislative authority has the power to make laws for the State." The provisions for the creation of legislation are set out in the respective standing orders of the Dáil and of the Seanad. This forms

---

[31] Such as UCD, UCC, NUIG, etc.
[32] See the candidates nominated for the Seanad Elections 2016 at https://www.oireachtas.ie/documents/publications/IRSup52b.pdf (accessed 9 February 2018).

part of the power of each House to make their own rules. The focus of the legislation is the creation of rules that will apply to future events rather than with the resolution of individual disputes. Legislation should be focused on the proactive creation of a framework of rules. However, some legislation can be created to react to problems within the State, such as some legislation created during the recent recession to deal with the protection of consumer deposits, the capitalisation of the banking sector and the reduction of State expenditure. The resolution of individual disputes is a function of the courts, and for the Oireachtas to step into this role would be transgressing the separation of powers.

Concerning the process itself, most Bills are initiated in the Dáil by the government, although it is permissible for Private Members' Bills to be initiated by TDs, and also for Bills to commence in the Seanad. There are five stages in the process of passing a Bill into law. When a Bill is passed through this stage and signed into law by the President, then the Bill is known as an Act of the Oireachtas. At Stage One, the Minister (in general) responsible circulates the Bill. Ministers of State may also circulate Bills. Private members are also able to circulate Bills where they are supported by seven TDs or five Senators and the Seanad leader. At Stage Two, the general provisions of the Bill will be debated. The Minister will present the government's case regarding the need for enactment of the legislation. The spokespersons for the other parties speak in response to the Minister and may either support or oppose the proposal. The opposition may seek to gather support to defeat the proposal. This rarely happens with government Bills. Stage Three is known as the Committee Stage. Here the Bill is debated section by section. As an alternative to the entire House sitting to discuss a Bill, a special or select committee can be formed to represent the House as a whole. The advantages of using a special committee is that the committee will consist of members with a special interest or expertise in the subject matter. Committees also free up parliamentary time to deal with other business. Stage Four is the Report Stage. The purpose of this stage is to review the work that has been conducted at the Committee Stage. Stage Five is the final stage and only verbal amendments are permissible at this stage. After this stage, no material changes may be made to the Bill and only spelling mistakes may be corrected.

It is important to note that where the Seanad does not pass a piece of legislation, unless it is an abridged time Bill, the legislation in question will be deemed to be passed after 180 days. Therefore, the Seanad does not have a veto on legislation but can only delay its passage under Art 23.1 An abridged time Bill is one where, due to emergency situations, the Seanad is by passed on the legislative process but any legislation passed in this manner has a limited period of operation of 90 days only under Art 24.3.

### 5.2.3.1 Delegated Legislation

This category of legislation may be referred to as subordinate or delegated legislation as well. Under the Constitution, only the Oireachtas has the power to make law for the State. Under Article 15.2.2° "[p]rovision may however be made by law for the creation or recognition of subordinate legislatures and for the powers and functions of these legislatures."

The power of a delegated body must be exercised in accordance with the Oireachtas and it may not usurp or step outside of the power delegated to it. Power must be expressly conferred on the delegate body, as it does not have any inherent law-making power of its own. The essential role for delegated legislation and the need for both parliamentary and court oversight was set out in *Cityview Press*,[33] as follows:

> "The giving of powers to a designated Minister or subordinate body to make regulations or orders under a particular statute has been a feature of legislation for many years. The practice has obvious attractions in view of the complex, intricate and ever-changing situations which confront both the Legislature and the Executive in a modern State. Sometimes, as in this instance, the legislature, conscious of the danger of giving too much power in the regulation or order-making process, provides that any regulation or order which is made should be subject to annulment by either House of Parliament. This retains a measure of control, if not in Parliament as such, at least in the two Houses. Therefore, it is a safeguard. Nevertheless, the ultimate responsibility rests with the Courts to ensure that constitutional safeguards remain, and that the exclusive authority of the National Parliament in the field of law-making is not eroded by a delegation of power which is neither contemplated nor permitted by the Constitution"[34]

The use of delegated legislation has grown with the expanding remit of local authorities, the rise in European legislation needing direct effect and the growth of government in general. The use of the committee system has helped to increase the efficacy of parliamentary time, yet

---

[33] *Cityview Press v An Chomhairle Oiliúna* [1980] IR 381.
[34] *ibid* at 389.

there is always growing demand on debate and participation in the chamber, so the use of the statutory instruments has been seen as a means of detailing practical measures. This leaves the Oireachtas free to legislate for general issues rather than specific concerns.

A statutory instrument is defined as an "order, regulation, rule, scheme or bye-law" under s 1(1) of the Statutory Instruments Act 1947 (the '1947 Act'). The 1947 Act also states the requirements for their printing, publishing and deposit in certain libraries and makes the publication of their effect compulsory in Iris Oifigiúil. This is a common-sense requirement. The volume of statutory instruments is so vast that there would have to be a central notification system to make people aware of their enforcement.

When the power to enact delegated legislation is vested in a Minister, then he must act within the powers of the granting document. For example, when the commencement date is not placed on a piece of legislation, then the Minister is able to bring the legislation into force by Ministerial Order. However, this power is only to bring the legislation into force, not to amend certain parts of the legislation. This can only be done by means of an amendment Act. Other areas where a Minister brings in delegated legislation would be in cases where a Minister is commencing the domestic legal effect of regulations or Directives from Europe.

Delegated legislation may also be used by local bodies. Many bodies such as former semi-state companies used delegated legislation as a means of regulating their service provision. For example, the use of public transport is governed by delegated legislation, such as the prohibition on alcohol on trains leaving Waterford over the weekends. City and county councils make wide use of delegated legislation in the form of managers' orders. Many persons who work in local government are appointed by means of a Manager's Order. Littering fines and parking regulations are also given force of law by means of delegated legislation.

The essential test to ascertain whether a body with delegated powers to make legislation is acting within their permitted parameters was set out in *Cityview Press v An Comhairle Oiliúna*.[35] O'Higgins CJ outlined the test as follows:

> "In the view of this Court, the test is whether that which is challenged as an unauthorised delegation of parliamentary power is more than a mere giving effect to principles

---

[35] [1980] IR 381.

and policies which are contained in the statute itself. If it be, then it is not authorised; for such would constitute a purported exercise of legislative power by an authority which is not permitted to do so under the Constitution. On the other hand, if it be within the permitted limits — if the law is laid down in the statute and details only are filled in or completed by the designated Minister or subordinate body — there is no unauthorised delegation of legislative power."[36]

If a body exceeds its powers in the creation of legislation or does not have the requisite powers to create legislation, then this legislation will have no legal effect. In *John Grace Fried Chicken v The Catering Joint Labour Committee*,[37] the court was asked to examine the power of the Joint Labour Committee (JLC) to create minimum rates of pay. The JLC system traditionally set minimum rates of pay for certain sectors outside of the provision of minimum wage legislation and even prior to the creation of a minimum wage framework. The claim of the plaintiff was that the legislation enabling the creation of the JLCs was did not "prescribe sufficient principles and policies to govern the exercise of the law making power" carried out in the statutory order which established the minimum rates of pay for those in the catering industry.[38] In setting out a detailed seventeen step list of "principles, factors and considerations to apply and take into account",[39] Feeney J held that the manner of the creation of the JLC rates of pay went beyond what was constitutionally permissible, stating that:

"a body which has delegated to it a power of subordinate legislation must exercise that power within the limitations which are expressed or necessarily implied in the provisions providing for such delegation. One implication which arises in the circumstances of such delegation is that the power to make subordinate legislation should be exercised reasonably. On the facts before this court that is not what has occurred. The Employment Regulation Order which was made introduced fixed wage rates and conditions of employment and was made in an arbitrary manner in that certain rates were set out for a geographical area when significantly different and more restrictive rates and conditions of employment applied in an immediate

---

36 *ibid* at 399.
37 [2011] 3 IR 211.
38 SI No 142 of 2008.
39 See [2011] 3 IR 211 at 227–229.

adjoining area without there being any identifiable basis for such discrimination."[40]

In *Bederev v Ireland*,[41] the plaintiff challenged the power of the government to criminalise specific drugs, in this case a drug called methylethcathinone, by means of subsidiary legislative action was constitutional. The provisions, however, were held to be unconstitutional as follows:

> "There can be no abrogation of the democratic responsibility of the Oireachtas to legislate by delegating undefined and unlimited powers of law-making either to Government or to any other body."[42]

### 5.2.4 Oireachtas Committees and Tribunals

There are two main roles for Oireachtas Committees. The first role is in relation to the legislative process referred to earlier, and the second is in relation to the examination of matters of public interest. The scope of Oireachtas Committees and tribunals is to find information and they cannot make adverse findings of fact.

#### 5.2.4.1 Oireachtas Committees

*Maguire v Ardagh*[43] was the seminal case examining the ability of the courts to uphold rights against the workings of the committees of the Oireachtas which required a fine line to be trodden between the roles of each organ under the doctrine of the separation of powers. The background to the *Maguire v Ardagh* concerned the operations of the Garda Emergency Response Unit in the wake of the death of John Carthy in Abbeylara. Mr Carthy was shot dead by members of the Garda during to an armed siege at his house. Mr Carthy's family wanted the Garda handling of the situation and the use of lethal force by the Gardaí examined. This case was to be the seminal case for delineating the boundaries of Oireachtas investigations. The wide-ranging judgment is summed up well by Doyle as follows:

---

[40] [2011] 3 IR 211 at 242.
[41] [2016] IESC 34.
[42] *ibid*, para 32. Also of note, Charleton J specifically referred to the constitutionality of statutory instruments in haste to deal with emergency problems as follows "While the State has argued urgency as a central factor justifying the delegation of legislative power, that cannot enable the abrogation of the power of the Oireachtas. The fact that a particular mischief, be it a financial crisis, the collapse of an insurance company or something similar, requires an urgent response does not justify any departure from the strict requirement that legislation is for the Oireachtas" [2016] IESC 34, para 25.
[43] [2002] 1 IR 385.

"A majority of the Supreme Court held that the Oireachtas has no inherent, general power to conduct an investigation. It was accepted by all parties that there was no explicit power to conduct investigations, but the respondents contented that there was an implicit power as such a power was necessary for the Oireachtas to function as a representative parliament."[44]

In essence, the judgment was concerned with the impact of the inquiry on the liability of individuals and findings affecting their good name. Such inquiries were political in nature, therefore there would be a risk that this political nature could affect the integrity and objectivity of the investigation. Even though the judgment implied narrow permissible grounds for inquiries, the Oireachtas now avoid any form of parliamentary investigation which may affect the good name of an individual.

The courts have also upheld this ground in the *Calleley*[45] case. Senator Callely sought judicial review in the High Court on the ability of the committee to make findings of fact and whether such findings were ultra vires, or outside the power of, the committee.[46] The background to the case consisted of two complaints by members of the public regarding the expenses claimed by the Senator which were referred to the Committee on Members' Interests of Seanad Éireann under the provisions of s 8 of the Ethics in Public Office Act 1995 (as amended by the Standards in Public Office Act 2001). A committee was convened to examine and investigate the complaints to see if there had been a breach of the legislation surrounding the claiming and recouping of expenses. The committee found that the Senator had not abided by the relevant rules and by resolution of the Seanad, he was prevented from partaking in its business for a number of days. Senator Callely then applied to the High Court for a declaration that the committee had acted outside of its powers in making such a resolution. The High Court agreed with the argument of the Senator, and held the Seanad had indeed overstepped its role as outlined in the Constitution by making a finding of fact regarding the complaint made against him.[47]

---

[44] O Doyle, *Constitutional Law: Text, Cases and Materials* (Clarus Press, Dublin, 2008), p 330.

[45] *Callely v Moylan* [2011] IEHC 2.

[46] The specific legal provisions in question were the Oireachtas (Allowances to Members) Act 1938, the Regulations adopted thereunder, being the Oireachtas (Allowances to Members) (Travelling Facilities and Overnight Allowances), Regulations 1998 (SI No 101 of 1998).

[47] This issue was also discussed in *Maguire v Ardagh* [2002] 1 IR 385 where the Supreme Court found that the Oireachtas overstepped its powers in making findings of fact which would impede on the good name of a citizen and the

Therefore, the resolution adopted by the Seanad from the "Report of the Results of an Investigation into Complaints Concerning Senator Ivor Callely" dated 14 July 2010 could be overturned by the court.

The finding that the committee and "the resolution of Seanad Éireann impugned in these proceedings were ultra vires the Acts of 1995 and 2001" was due to the committee failing

> "to exercise their adjudicative function in an appropriate judicial manner by making a political judgment on the issues in the investigation, thereby breaching the applicant's constitutional right to natural justice and fair procedures."[48]

The *Callely* judgment emphasised that the courts must still uphold the basics of natural justice—in this particular instance, the right to defend oneself.

However, the intervention of the court in this case has to be contrasted to the parliamentary privilege cases of *O'Brien*[49] and *Keirns*,[50] where they were unable to intervene, as the central issue was parliamentary privilege and not the adherence to constitutional natural rights. The Courts were able to intervene in the *Callely* case, as they were upholding the rights of individuals against the process of the Oireachtas committee. In the parliamentary privilege cases, the individuals were seeking the court to intervene in the statements and opinions of members of the Oireachtas which are protected under the doctrine of parliamentary privilege.

### 5.2.4.2 Tribunals

Under the provisions of Art 37, the Oireachtas may pass legislation for the establishment of tribunals which allows for

> "limited functions and powers of a judicial nature, in matters other than criminal matters, by any person or body of person duly authorised by law to exercise such functions and powers".[51]

The governing law for tribunals in Ireland is the Tribunal of Enquiries (Evidence) Act 1921. There have been various amendments

drafters of the Houses of the Oireachtas (Inquiries, Privileges and Procedures) Bill 2013 have tried to reflect this in constructing the relevant clauses.
48 Judgment of O'Neill J in *Callely v Moylan* [2011] IEHC 2, para. 122.
49 [2017] IEHC 179.
50 [2017] IEHC 34 and also see parliamentary privilege at section 5.2.6.
51 Art 37.1.

emanating from experiences in recent tribunals.[52] The primary function of a tribunal is to investigate facts in the public interest and not to administer justice. Some Tribunals are established by statute and others by ministerial decision; therefore they are subject to the provisions of administrative law when exercising their powers. The chair of the tribunal is mandated by the Oireachtas and the powers and procedures of such tribunals are set out in the establishing legislation. Tribunals are vested with the privileges and rights of the High Court in relation to non-co-operative witnesses and are said to be clothed with the powers of the High Court as they have statutory powers to enforce attendance and examination and the production of relevant documents. However, they are not able to make findings of non-co-operation against witnesses but must send them before the High Court otherwise, as bodies set up by the Oireachtas, they would be in violation of the doctrine of the separation of powers. They differ from parliamentary enquiries as parliamentary enquiries are on a non-statutory basis and are not vested with the privileges and rights of the High Court.

### 5.2.5 Attempt to Create Oireachtas Inquiries

In the wake of the *Maguire v Ardagh* case and its fallout, the Oireachtas Joint Committee on the Constitution recommended that the Constitution be amended to give greater powers to both create Oireachtas Inquiries as an alternative to the use of Tribunals and Oireachtas Committees for investigating issues. The 30th Amendment to the Constitution was proposed in 2011 in order to extend the powers of the Oireachtas in this regard. The proposed amendment would have allowed for each House to have the power to conduct inquiries and to make findings against persons subject to inquiry.[53] The referendum

---

[52] For example, experience gained in the running of the Flood Tribunal with reference to the variation of the terms of reference resulted in the Tribunal of Enquiries (Evidence) Amendment Act 1997.

[53] The full list of proposed amendments to Art 15.10 were as follows:

"2° Each House shall have the power to conduct an inquiry, or an inquiry with the other House, in a manner provided for by law, into any matter stated by the House or Houses concerned to be of general public importance.

3° In the course of any such inquiry the conduct of any person (whether or not a member of either House) may be investigated and the House or Houses concerned may make findings in respect of the conduct of that person concerning the matter to which the inquiry relates.

4° It shall be for the House or Houses concerned to determine, with due regard to the principles of fair procedures, the appropriate balance between the rights of persons and the public interest for the purposes of ensuring an effective inquiry into any matter to which subsection 2° applies."

was held alongside the 2011 Presidential Election and was rejected by the people.

### 5.2.6 Parliamentary Privilege

The chamber of Dáil Éireann is envisaged as the central venue for the debate of matters of public importance and the most powerful chamber for the debate of legislation.[54] In order to adhere to this role, it is essential that the directly-elected deputies are facilitated by both the internal rules of debate, known as standing orders, and the constitutional provisions creating the framework for free debate. Members of both Houses are protected from defamation law by means of privilege. However, this may create instances where persons outside the Oireachtas believe that their reputation has been tarnished with no means of redress. Parliamentary privilege is a constitutional right granted to the elected members in the exercise of their democratic role as representatives of their constituents. Parliamentary privilege is a legal safeguard that protects their statements in the Oireachtas from being scrutinised by a court as stated in Art 15.13 granting constitutional protection to statements made in parliament and s 17 of the Defamation Act 2009 which establishes the defence of absolute privilege. However, if the statements made in parliament are found to contain utterances that are defamatory, it may affect a person's reputation, but the absolute nature of this speech right may leave a person with no remedy in court and no means to clear their name or seek redress. The courts cannot enter this territory, as their intervention in the legislative or executive domain is prohibited by the theory of separation of powers. Therefore, the only recourse open to a citizen is via standing order procedures that allow for the Committee on Privileges and Procedures and the Ceann Chomhairle to review the comments made.

The concept of parliamentary privilege refers to the degree of judicial scrutiny that can be applied to the proceedings of Parliament and the utterances of its members. For the sake of democracy, the power of judicial scrutiny in the business of parliament is fettered to the extreme to preserve the constitutional theory of separation of powers. It allows for members to discuss and debate issues of national importance without any chilling effect which may emanate from legal interference with the to and fro of debate.

---

[54] Some minor changes were recommended to the internal regulations governing parliamentary privilege in a recent report commissioned by the Ceann Comhairle such as extending the time limit for making complaints. *http://opac. oireachtas.ie/AWDatu/Library3/Parliamentary_privilege_report_for_laying_222040. pdf* [accessed 10 April 2018].

From Bunreacht na hÉireann 1937, it is quite clear that the privilege granted to its members is to allow them to carry out their powers in the pursuit of democracy. The overwhelming public interest in unfettered debate in parliament is a counterbalance to any damage to an individual's interest in their right to a good name.[55]. The Defamation Act 2009 reinforced the already clear legal situation as laid down in the Constitution.[56] Absolute privilege is recognition of the desirability of allowing for full and unfettered speech on issues of public concern in the chamber. This means that any court cannot scrutinise any statements of an alleged defamatory nature. With regard to the Houses of the Oireachtas (Inquiries, Privileges and Procedures) Bill 2013, the Defamation Act states that witnesses before current committees and Dáil-mandated tribunals, commissions of inquiry or investigations are covered by absolute privilege and any protection offered by the relevant legislation.

Two cases have examined the powers of parliamentary privilege in both committees and in the Dáil. In both *O'Brien v Clerk of the Dáil*[57] and *Kerins v McGuinness*,[58] the ability of the courts to scrutinise statements made in the Oireachtas, either in the chamber or in committees, was clearly dealt with. The courts are unable to review such statements, regardless of the nature, scope or reason for the statements, as it is stated clearly in the Constitution that parliamentary privilege does not allow for the courts to intervene. If the courts did intervene, they would be in violation of the doctrine of the separation of powers.

### 5.2.7 The Electoral Process

The process of elections in Ireland is covered in Art 16. Article 16.2.1° sets out the Constituency basis for election and Art 16.2.2° sets out the representation ratio between members of the Dáil in relation to the number of citizens. The constituencies for the Dáil will be determined by law but with no less than one member per each 30,000

---

[55] Art 15.10 states that the Dáil and Seanad has the power to "make its own rules and standing orders, ... power to ensure freedom of debate ... and to protect itself and its members against any person or persons interfering with, molesting or attempting to corrupt its members in the exercise of their duties." Therefore, it is clear that freedom of debate is of extreme importance to the nature of democracy in Ireland. Moreover, the provisions of Art 15.12 add more weight to the privilege afforded to Members of the Oireachtas in their deliberations in the Chamber, stating that "All official reports and publications of the Oireachtas or of either House thereof and utterances made in either House wherever published shall be privileged".

[56] s 17 contains the defence of absolute privilege for defamatory statements made in either Chamber of the Oireachtas.

[57] [2017] IEHC 179.

[58] [2017] IEHC 34.

persons. The representative ratio will be kept as far as practicable even between constituencies. This was not the case in *O'Donovan v Attorney General*,[59] where the practice of allocating more representation to rural constituencies was deemed to be repugnant to the Constitution thereby creating the "one vote, one value", rule as stated by Gwynn Morgan.[60] Constituencies will be based on the previous census and will be reviewed once every twelve years. However, any changes will take place at the next general election. Each constituency will return at least three members. Members will be elected on the basis of proportional representation by a single transferable vote.[61] There have already been two failed referenda to change the system in both 1958 and 1968 when it was proposed to change the electoral system from the current proportional representation system to the first past the post system.

The first legislative enactment to deal with electoral integrity was the Electoral Act 1923. This was the first piece of legislation aimed at promoting integrity in the electoral system by the new State and varied and repealed previous enactments relating to Irish elections from the Parliamentary Elections (Ireland) Act 1850. The Schedules of the Act also contained the structure and regulated contents of official paperwork from the structure of the ballot paper to the Public Notice of the Result of the Election and of the Transfer of Votes. The Prevention of Electoral Abuses Act 1923 contained the definition of a number of electoral offences and their statutory punishment to ensure the integrity of the electoral process. These offences included corrupt practices, bribery, personation, threats and undue influence. This Act also set out the powers and roles of the election agent. Both of these Acts were repealed by the Electoral Act 1992 (the '1992 Act'). The 1992 Act was to form a new landscape for the regulation of elections from franchise and registration of electors through to electoral offences. The Acts that follow on from the 1992 Act can all be considered as amendment Acts. Such amendments were required for various reasons such as: increasing the number of members in the

---

[59] [1961] IR 114.

[60] D Gwynn Morgan, *Administrative Law in Ireland* (4th ed, Round Hall, Dublin, 2012), p 224.

[61] The Constitution also sets out the rules for election to the Seanad in Art 18. The rules for eligibility are the same as the Dáil. However, the mechanics of election are different than those set down for the Dáil as there is a fundamentally different constituency basis for Seanad elections, such as university constituencies, Taoiseach's nominees and panels.

Dáil,[62] reflecting changes in EU parliament elections,[63] constituency boundary amendments[64] and prisoner voting rights,[65] amongst others.

Some of the amendments have been purely reactionary, such as the most recent amendment, which filled in a gap where there was an absence, incapacity or vacancy in office of Clerk of Dáil Éireann that made the fulfilment of certain roles and responsibilities impossible. The Electoral (Amendment) (No 2) Act 2014 allows for the clerk-assistant to fill in such a situation. The Electoral (Amendment) Act 2011 was enacted to allow for a streamlined and more efficient process for the holding of bye-elections. The new legislation allows for the Chairman of the Dáil to direct the clerk to issue a writ to the Returning Officer for the constituency affected to hold a bye-election if the Dáil has not already voted to do so within a six month timeframe. This can be seen as a direct reaction to the court challenges that were taken against the previous government regarding the delay in holding bye-elections.[66] Some electoral legislation has proved to be a disaster. For example, the Electoral (Amendment) Acts 2001 and 2004 were passed to both consider and run electronic voting machines in some constituencies, and was originally an attempt to modernise the current electoral processes, but in the end was a costly failure and only used in selected constituencies in one general election.

In the Art 26[67] reference of the Electoral Amendment Bill 1983, the general provisions of electoral legislation were contrasted to the constitutional provisions which act as the bedrock regulation. O'Higgins CJ stated that the constitutional provisions in Art 16 "indicate a total code for the holding of elections to Dáil Éireann, setting out the matters which would appear to be necessary other than minor regulatory provisions."[68] In this case, the provisions to extend Dáil voting privilege to UK nationals by legislation were deemed unconstitutional. However, the provisions were enacted by means of the 9th Amendment to the Constitution. Higgins CJ also listed the provisions of electoral regulations that were set out in the

[62] Electoral (Amendment) (No 2) Act 1998.
[63] Electoral (Amendment) Act 2002.
[64] Electoral (Amendment) Act 2005.
[65] Electoral (Amendment) Act 2006.
[66] E.g. in *Doherty v An Taoiseach* [2010] IEHC 369.
[67] An Art 26 reference allows for the Supreme Court to have a hypothetical argument regarding the constitutionality of proposed legislation. This provision is commenced by the President referring legislation requiring presidential assent to the Supreme Court for adjudication after consultation with the Council of State. The main issue with such legislation is that its constitutionality can never be tested again by a court.
[68] *In Re the Electoral (Amendment) Bill 1983* [1984] 1 IR 268, 274.

Constitution.[69] He then contrasted this list of constitutional electoral regulation to issues which were to be considered as minor regulatory provisions.[70]

The primary right to vote is found in Art 16. Article 16.1.1° states that all citizens over the age of 18 without reference to gender and without disability or incapacity are entitled to vote in Dáil elections. This right extends to all elections, including presidential elections, and to all referendums. Since the 9th Amendment to the Constitution in 1984, UK nationals can vote in Dáil elections. The right to vote for second-order elections, such as European parliament elections and local elections has been extended. UK citizens are entitled to vote in all Dáil, European and local elections, all other EU citizens are entitled to vote in European and local elections and non-nationals are entitled to vote in local elections only.

---

[69] "These other provisions of that Article (1) prohibit the enactment of any law placing a citizen under disability or incapacity for membership of Dáil Éireann on the grounds of sex, or disqualifying on the same grounds any citizen from voting at an election for Dáil Éireann; (2) prohibit the exercise by any voter of more than one vote at an election for Dáil Éireann; (3) provide for the secrecy of the ballot; (4) provide for the ratio between members of Dáil Éireann and the population; (5) impose upon the Oireachtas an obligation to revise constituencies at least once in every 12 years, with due regard to changes in distribution of the population; (6) provide for elections to be on the system of proportional representation by means of the single transferable vote; (7) prohibit the enactment of any law providing for the number of members to be returned for any constituency being less than three; (8) provide that a general election shall take place not later than 30 days after the dissolution of Dáil Éireann; (9) provide that the same Dáil Éireann shall not continue for a longer period than seven years from the date of its first meeting; (10) provide that polling at every election for Dáil Éireann shall, as far as practicable, take place on the same day throughout the country; (11) impose an obligation to make provision by law to enable the member of Dáil Éireann who is the chairman immediately before the dissolution to be deemed, without any actual election, to be elected a member of Dáil Éireann at the ensuing general election; and (12) finally, by Article 16, s. 7, they provide that, subject to the foregoing provisions, elections for membership of Dáil Éireann' including the filling of casual vacancies, shall be regulated in accordance with law." *In Re The Electoral (Amendment) Bill, 1983* [1984] 1 IR 268 at 274.

[70] "In contrast with this code of essential features of elections for Dáil Éireann, the matters which are left to be regulated by law would appear to be (a) the disqualification of citizens from voting; (b) the provisions with which citizens must comply in order to have the right to vote; (c) the fixing of the number of members of Dáil Éireann within the ratio laid down by the Constitution; (d) the provision, subject to the minimum of three, of the number of members for each constituency; (e) the fixing of the date of a general election subject to a restriction as to the maximum period after the dissolution of the Dáil; (f) the period during which the same Dáil may continue subject to the constitutional maximum of seven years; and (g) the details of the mandatory provision for the re-election of the chairman of Dáil Éireann". *In Re The Electoral (Amendment) Bill, 1983* [1984] 1 IR 268 at 275.

Under the provisions of this Article every citizen over the age of 21, without distinction of sex and without any disability or incapacity under law, is eligible to run for office. The issue of legal incapacity to run is set out in s 51(2) of the Electoral Act of 1923 and s 41 of the Electoral Act 1992. Those who are considered to fall foul of such provisions would be a person who is not an Irish citizen, a person who is a member of the Commission of the EU, a judge, advocate general or registrar of the EU courts, a member of the Court of Auditors of the EU, member of the Gardaí or whole-time member of the Defence Forces,[71] members of the civil service who are prevented from being a member of the Dáil as part of their terms of employment,[72] a person who is serving a term of imprisonment for more than six months[73] and a person of unsound mind.[74] Additionally, the President, Auditor and Comptroller General and Attorney General cannot stand for election under Arts 12.6, 33.3 and 35.3 respectively. Previously under the provisions of s 41 of the Electoral Act 1992, an undischarged bankrupt under adjudication by a court in the Irish jurisdiction would be deemed ineligible for election to the Dáil. This position allowed for a time period of six months for the bankruptcy to be discharged. If this did not happen within this time period, then under the provisions of the Bankruptcy Act 1988, s 85(7), the member would forfeit his seat and a vacancy would be declared. The provisions for bankrupts have recently been amended by the removal of s 41(k), which prevented an undischarged bankrupt from being a member of the Dáil.

---

[71] The imposition of disqualification on the grounds of membership of either the Gardaí or whole-time member of the Defence Forces is due to their role in upholding State security. It was mentioned by Barrington J in *Aughney v Ireland* [1986] ILRM 206 that due to their close connection with the security of the State that they have different limitations placed on their constitutional rights than other citizens.

[72] G Hogan and G Whyte, *JM Kelly: The Irish Constitution* (4th ed, Tottel Publishing, Dublin, 2006), p 311 argue that this restriction is legitimate as it would be "incongruous (if not destructive of the relationship of trust which must exist between Minister and his civil servants advisors) of a senior civil servant could stand for election, even perhaps in the self-same constituency as his Minister". However, under the provisions of the civil service circular, it is stated that following a government decision of 1985, there is no prohibition on the political life of special advisors. However, "Personal Secretaries, Civilian Drivers and any other personal appointees of Ministers, Ministers of State, Parliamentary office holders and the Attorney General may also engage in political activity and contest local elections. However, such persons are not permitted to stand for election to either House of the Oireachtas or the European Parliament unless permitted to do so by the terms of their contract" (Department of Finance, Circular 9/2009).

[73] G Hogan and G Whyte, *JM Kelly: The Irish Constitution* (4th ed, Tottel Publishing, Dublin, 2006), p 311 commented that such a restriction regarding prisoner voting may be questionable on constitutional grounds.

[74] G Hogan and G Whyte, *JM Kelly: The Irish Constitution* (4th ed, Tottel Publishing, Dublin, 2006), p 331.

In the case of *Redmond v Minister for the Environment*,[75] the issue of conditions on the candidature for Dáil elections was addressed. In this case, the applicant questioned the conditions which were put on candidates, in this instance, the requirement of a deposit to be paid. Herbert J stated that the

> "limited right of citizens to be electable to membership of Dáil Éireann is thus clearly identified as deriving from and constituting an essential feature of (Article 16) and not from any regulatory laws authorised by Article 16."[76]

The right of citizens to participate in government is derived from Art 5 of the Constitution and therefore any power to place a citizen under a disability or incapacity to seek membership of Dáil Éireann must be limited.[77] Herbert J also emphasised that Art 16.7 conferred no more than a right to regulate elections in line with the constitutional provisions contained within the entirety of Art 16.[78] In spite of the hard line that was taken by the court in finding the provision unconstitutional, the deposit measure was more of an overly burdensome means of regulating elections, rather than an attempt at preventing persons from seeking election. However, this judgment does demonstrate that the courts are active in upholding rights of citizens who believe that their constitutional right to run as a candidate is being infringed.

Alternative provisions were put in place to allow for a system of assenters. These provisions were then questioned in the case of *King v Minister for the Environment (No. 2)*,[79] where one of the disparities

---

[75] [2001] 4 IR 61.

[76] *ibid* at 77.

[77] Furthermore, gender quotas have been introduced in the Electoral (Amendment) (Political Funding) Act 2012 with a view to financially incentivise political parties to run an increased amount of female candidates in the next General Election. The objective of the legislation is to have registered political parties run women candidates as over 33 percent of their overall candidates. If this objective is not achieved, then the registered parties will receive a reduced amount of central government financial support for the next Dáil term. Many criticised this measure as it could be argued to discriminate against prospective male candidates. However, as the legislation is set out as a financial incentivisation scheme, it is hard to see how critics can claim that the measure inhibits men from running as candidates. There is nothing preventing men running as independent candidates, and as previously stated, there is no constitutional protection for political parties. There is therefore no constitutional right of a political party being transgressed when such gender quota measures are being exercised. Only if the personal right of a citizen to run as a candidate in an independent nature was being restricted would such legislation be constitutionally questionable.

[78] [2001] 4 IR 61 at 78.

[79] [2007] IR 296.

between being a party candidate and non-party candidate was highlighted. The applicant in this case questioned the need for non-party candidates to collect the names of 30 assenters while a party candidate did not need to gather such assents once they were the selected candidate by the political party. In the Supreme Court judgment, it was held that there was a rational basis for such discrimination as both procedures were to show a minimum level of commitment to the political process.

The right to a postal vote is not extended to emigrants and according to Hogan and Whyte,[80] it may be unconstitutional to do so unless there is a successful referendum to insert this provision into the Constitution.

Section 37 of the Electoral Act 1992 states that a transferable vote is one which indicates the voter's preference in order and can be transferred to the next choice "when the vote is not required to give a prior choice the necessary quota of votes, or when, owing to the deficiency in the number of the votes given for a prior choice, that choice is excluded from the list of candidates." In the judgment of O'Donnell J in *Kiely v Kerry County Council*[81]:

> "Proportional representation is a notoriously sensitive system and the outcome of an election may depend not just on the numbers, the votes, and the preferences, but also on the sequence in which they are distributed. Even if on their face the removal of invalid votes might appear broadly neutral, their removal may have an impact on the distribution of votes, the elimination of candidates, and therefore the election of others."[82]

The voting system itself is set out in the Constitution in Art 12.5, which states that "The members shall be elected on the system of proportional representation by means of the single transferable vote." The members will be returned on constituency basis under the provisions of Art 12.1. No less than three members may be returned per constituency as per Art 12.6. The remainder of Art 12 sets out the minimum criteria for election to the Dáil. The most important aspect of the minimum criteria is the establishment of a representation ratio for members of the Dáil per head of population. This is set at one member per 20,000 to 30,000 head of population. These numbers will be set on the basis of the previous census and should be kept as constant as possible

---

[80] G Hogan and G Whyte, *JM Kelly: The Irish Constitution* (4th ed, Tottel Publishing, Dublin, 2006), p 317.

[81] *Kiely v Kerry County Council* [2015] IESC 97.

[82] *ibid*, para. 10

between different constituencies. Constituencies will be revised every 12 years. The most recent Constituency Commission reported in 2012 on the basis of the 2011 census.[83] This was the fourth Commission established under the terms of the Electoral Act 1997 in order to fulfil the provisions of the Constitution. The Constitution does permit for the number of members of Dáil Éireann to be regulated by law.[84]

Article 16.4.1° states that polling for Dáil elections will take place on the same date throughout the country where practicable. However, there are three main exemptions: postal voters and special voters will vote in advance of the general polling date to allow for the return of their ballot papers, and voting on the islands. Pursuant to s 85 of the Electoral Act 1992, voting can take place in advance on the islands due to transport or weather difficulties. Also under s 62 of that Act, the date of the poll can be varied. The provisions of Art 16.4 state that there is only one vote per elector and the vote is by means of a secret ballot. This provision regarding secrecy was used in *McMahon v Attorney General*[85] to find the provisions of s 26 of the Electoral Act of 1923 unconstitutional as the system of numbering votes could undermine the secrecy of the ballot. The provision in question stated that the back of each ballot paper had to be numbered consecutively. This number was on the front of the counterfoil and the electoral number of the voter had to be marked on the counterfoil. This meant that it was possible for the voter and the ballot to be identified. The applicant successfully argued that the totality of these provisions undermined the secrecy of the ballot.

The provisions of ss 137 and 162 of the Electoral Act 1992 also places duties of secrecy both on those who are voting and present at the opening of ballot boxes. Under s 137 an offence is committed if a person communicates, before the poll is closed, the official mark, the number on the back of any ballot paper, details on the electoral register, or the identities of those that have voted. The section also criminalises interfering with voters while voting, communicating the number on the back of the ballot paper, causing someone to display their marked ballot or interfering with the return of a ballot paper. Thus, the practice of taking photos of marked ballots and placing them on social media could be considered to be a criminal offence. Section 162

---

[83] Constituency Commission, *Report on Dáil and European Parliament Constituencies* (2012).

[84] The Electoral (Amendment) (Dáil Constituencies) Act 2013 has now reduced the number of members for the current Dáil to 158. The revised constituencies for the reduced Dáil are set out in the Schedule to the Act. However, this number is now too low for the increased population of Ireland since the last census, so the number of TDs must be increased for the next General Election.

[85] [1972] IR 69.

also reaffirmed the secrecy of the ballot and s 163 states that at legal proceedings no voter can be required to state how they voted or for which candidate. This demonstrates that the rules related to electoral offences are quite specific.

From *Dudley v An Taoiseach*[86] to the recent case of *Doherty v Ireland*,[87] there have been issues regarding delays with bye-elections to fill casual vacancies. In *Dudley*, the applicant complained that an inordinate delay—fourteen months—in the holding of a bye-election affected his constitutional rights, and sought judicial review of the actions of the respondent parties. The constitutional right directly mentioned was the right to vote. Due to the drafting of the Electoral Act 1992, the procedure for a bye-election is started when the Dáil agrees to a motion to hold the bye-election thereby directing the clerk of the Dáil to set in train the procedures for a bye-election. In *Doherty*, Hogan J specifically links the sovereign independent nature of the democratic State as laid down in Art 5 as the linchpin of democratic representation stated in Art 16.1, adding that it "set out the citizens' rights in clear and unambiguous terms".[88] In *Doherty*, even though the court was constrained by the operation of the separation of powers doctrine, it was willing to intervene due to the degree and the duration of the interference. However, with the passage of the Electoral (Amendment) Act 2013, a writ to hold a bye-elections will now be automatically issued by the Clerk of the Dáil if the Dáil has failed to move the writ after six months of the vacancy arising.

## 5.3 The Executive

The executive is better known as the cabinet. The cabinet comprises of the Taoiseach, Tánaiste and the Ministers. There cannot be more than 15 members of the cabinet and they are appointed by the President. These members exercise the executive power of the State in respect of their departments' scope and functions. Ministers of State do not sit at cabinet. The Attorney General sits at cabinet as a legal advisor to the executive but does not have a vote.[89]

The government is responsible to the Dáil and meets as a collective authority. The confidentiality of government meetings is to be respected unless the High Court determines that it should be lifted in the interests of the administration of justice, by reason of an overwhelming public interest and where a tribunal requests such

---

[86] [1994] 2 ILRM 321.
[87] [2010] IEHC 369.
[88] *ibid*, para 47.
[89] See the provisions relating to the Attorney General in section 5.4.1.

information. This provision was inserted in the wake of the *Hamilton* case where the courts disproportionally favoured the confidentiality of government meeting irrespective of the public interest in the release of such information.[90]

The head of the government is to be known as the Taoiseach and is to keep the President informed on matters of domestic and international policy. The Taoiseach is then to nominate the Tánaiste who will act in place of the Taoiseach during periods of temporary absence, illness, death, or permanent incapacitation. The Taoiseach, Tánaiste and Minister for Finance must be members of the Dáil. It is possible for the Taoiseach to appoint not more than two Seanad members to cabinet. Ministers have a right to attend and be heard in both Houses. The Taoiseach may resign by placing his resignation in the hands of the President. Other members of the cabinet may resign in a similar manner. The President shall accept this resignation if advised by the Taoiseach. The Taoiseach can ask a Minister to resign, and if they do not comply then the appointment will be terminated by the President on the Taoiseach's advice. The Taoiseach will resign from Office when he or she fails to retain the support of the majority of the Dáil. If the Taoiseach resigns, then other members of the cabinet will be deemed to have resigned also, but they will continue their duties until their successors have been appointed. This situation is similar when the Dáil is dissolved for general election.

In times of war, the State shall not participate in any war unless the Dáil assents. In the case of an invasion, the government as the executive can take any measure considered necessary to protect the State. In such an instance, the Dáil will be convened to sit as soon as possible if it is not already in session. Article 28.3 also sets down the powers which may be used to protect the State in a time of war or armed rebellion. This provision is known as the emergency provisions article and allows for laws to remain in force regardless of their constitutionality, apart from allowing for the death penalty.

The concept of 'Cabinet' as an organ of government developed in the Westminster-style organisation of governmental functions. This point was made by Farrell in his article on "Constitution and the Institutions of Government: Constitutional Theory and Political Practice", stating that the cabinet model adapted for use in Ireland was directly inherited from the English system and was adopted in 1919 "without any serious examination of its appropriateness to local conditions".[91] This

---

90  [1993] 2 IR 250.
91  B Farrell, "The Constitution and the Institutions of Government: Constitutional Theory and Political Practice" (1987) 35(4) *Administration* 169.

is also a point that is taken up by Basil Chubb in *The Constitution and Constitutional Change in Ireland,* stating that the "British type cabinet system was to become firmly established as tentative moves towards parliamentary governance failed".[92]

### 5.3.1 Cabinet Confidentiality

Cabinet confidentiality seeks to preserve the confidentiality of cabinet discussions. The central claim behind the need for cabinet confidentiality is that the executive needs the ability to act in a collective manner and this collective manner is predicated on the ability to preserve the confidentiality of meetings. Cabinet confidentiality means that discussion of cabinet meetings is deemed as confidential and minutes of such meetings are kept confidential for a period of 30 years under the National Archives Act 1998. Thus, the discussions of topical issues, such as the bank bailout, are kept hidden from the general public for 30 years.

The case *of Murphy v Corporation of Dublin*[93] established that where a conflict arose between the protection of executive privilege and the release of information in the public interest, the judiciary must decide the best course of action. Walsh J stated that the judiciary had the right to decide which public interest shall prevail,[94] adding that it was impossible for any other power or body to decide whether or not a document should be disclosed or produced.[95] Even in circumstances where the security of the State was in question, the court should and could make its own decision, and although it would be open to being guided by the circumstances of the case, "the division of powers does not give paramountcy in all circumstances to any one of the organs of state."[96] In *Ambiorix Ltd v Minister for the Environment,*[97] the argument of the Taoiseach and ministers of the day was rejected. Their argument that the disclosure of documents would tend to hinder the free communications necessary for government and the running of the public service was not persuasive.

However, *Attorney General v Hamilton*[98] swung the established precedents towards undue deference of the government. The judgment and subsequent political fallout was to act as the catalyst for the

---

[92] B Chubb, *The Constitution and Constitutional Change in Ireland* (IPA, Dublin, 1978), p 10.
[93] [1972] IR 215.
[94] *ibid* at 233.
[95] *ibid* at 234.
[96] [1972] IR 215 at 234.
[97] [1992] 1 IR 277.
[98] [1993] ILRM 81.

1997 referendum on cabinet confidentiality. The key issue was the legitimacy of the claim of absolute privilege which was asserted over documents relating to the beef industry of the day, which therefore pertained to the consequent tribunal. In the High Court, O'Hanlon J held that a proper balance had to be maintained between the public interest of confidentiality, the public interest in obtaining full disclosure and the rights of the individual as guaranteed by the Constitution. Having regard to the absence of any express words providing for such confidentiality in the Constitution itself, the public interest did not require the upholding of such a claim of absolute confidentiality. Therefore, there were legitimate reasons for the tribunal to seek, and be granted, the documentation surrounding the cabinet meeting of 8 June 1988.

In the Supreme Court, McCarthy J and Egan J dissented from the majority on the cabinet confidentiality issue, holding that the correct test had been applied in the High Court when the requirements of a parliamentary inquiry were balanced with the requirements of confidential communications at government level. However, the majority decision of the court in *Hamilton* created an absolute privilege for the decisions of the cabinet. As stated by Finlay CJ, the:

> "claim for confidentiality of the contents and details of discussions at meetings of the government, ... is a valid claim. It extends to discussions and to their contents, but it does not, of course, extend to the decisions made and the documentary evidence of them, whether they are classified as formal or informal decisions. It is a constitutional right (that) goes to the fundamental machinery of government, and is ... not capable of being waived by any individual member of a government, nor ... are the details and contents of discussions at meetings of the government capable of being made public, ... by a decision of any succeeding government."[99]

The effect of the *Hamilton* judgment was to throw any system of oversight on the running of government into disarray.[100] It meant that as no judicial body in the land could scrutinise a claim from the executive that the release of essential documents for the administration of justice could not be entertained. Not only were the documents

---

[99] [1993] ILRM 81 at 100.
[100] One of the first implications of the judgment was the release of government papers under the thirty year rule of the National Archives Act. The Taoiseach of the day, Charles Haughey, had to personally sign off on the release of the documents at Christmas 1992. The Taoiseach claimed to exercise this power as this thirty year rule was not considered in the *Hamilton* judgment.

protected by a 30 year rule for general release, even where they were required by a body established in the public interest, they could not be accessed when said documents referred to a policy decision of the day. A referendum to modify the decision was promised by the Rainbow Coalition in their Programme for Government, stating that "relaxation of absolute confidence in all circumstances will be put to the people".[101] This provision was passed and Article 28.4.3° was inserted to the Constitution to provide for safeguards to override cabinet confidentiality on application to the High Court either in the interests of the administration of justice or where there is an overriding public interest.[102]

The position of accessing such information in the wake of the *Hamilton*[103] judgment and the 17th Amendment of the Constitution has received little attention. The case of *Irish Press Publications v Minister for Enterprise and Employment*[104] highlighted the implications of the *Hamilton* decision. In this case, the plaintiffs were suing for libel, negligence and wrongful interference with their constitutional right to a good name in the wake of the closure of the Irish Press. Amongst the items sought in discovery, the plaintiffs wanted to access some government documents dealing with the closure. The State sought to preclude the release of these documents, claiming they were covered by cabinet confidentiality. In the consideration of the issues in the High Court, Carroll J stated that as the range of documents covered both communications and documents prepared for cabinet, a number of considerations had to be made. Regarding one of the documents which was a communication from a private secretary, the umbrella term of cabinet confidentiality did not apply as it was the only ground pleaded. In relation to other documents sought, Carroll J was cognisant of the administration of justice and unjust disadvantage as these were cabinet documents.

> "In my view, the administration of justice would not be compromised in any way by upholding the defendant's claim to privilege on the grounds of cabinet confidentiality.

---

[101] *A Government for Renewal: Programme for Government for the Fine Gael, Labour and Democratic Left 1994–1997* (Stationery Office, Dublin, 1994), p 32.

[102] The Article states that "the confidentiality of discussions at meetings of the Government shall be respected in all circumstances save only where the High Court determines that disclosure should be made in respect of a particular manner in the interests of the administration of justice by a court, or by virtue of an overriding public interest, pursuant to an application in that behalf ... to inquire into a matter stated by them to be of public importance".

[103] *Attorney General v Hamilton* [1993] ILRM 81.

[104] *Irish Press Publications v Minister for Enterprise and Employment* [2002] 4 IR 110.

I am satisfied that the plaintiffs would not be unjustly disadvantaged by allowing this claim for privilege".[105]

In *Minister for Education and Science v Information Commissioner*,[106] McGovern J in the High Court, was asked to interpret the provisions of s 28(1) regarding cabinet documents. The Information Commissioner sought documentation regarding the contribution of religious orders to the residential institutions redress scheme from a document which was prepared for cabinet. The Information Commissioner argued that the documents were prepared for the purposes of information and should therefore be subject to the provisions of the Freedom of Information Acts.[107] Furthermore, these documents were not used primarily for conducting the business of State. The High Court held that the document was prepared and created for the purpose of being submitted to government and allowing access to the document could have implications. These implications listed by McGovern J were that documents containing ministerial advice could be disclosed; this could undermine government confidence and would strike at the constitutionally enshrined doctrine of collective responsibility. However, McGovern J did add that the exemption of documents should only occur in exceptional circumstances, as the public should not be deprived of information held.

## 5.4 Constitutional Office Holders

There are a number of other office holders that are detailed in the Constitution. These are the Attorney General and the Comptroller and Auditor General. Both of these roles are essential to the workings of the government and therefore their powers and role are set out in the Constitution. The Attorney General is the legal adviser to the State and the Comptroller and Auditor General is the main auditor for State expenditure and seeking value for money for the expenditure of the State.

### 5.4.1 Attorney General

The Attorney General is appointed under the provisions of Art 30 to act as the legal adviser to the government in all matters in law and

---

[105] [2002] 4 IR 110 at 116 and referencing *Bula Mines v Tara Mines Ltd (No.4)* [1991] 1 IR 217 regarding the duty of the defendant to list documents sought in discovery to allow the plaintiff to determine whether any claim for privilege is properly maintained.

[106] *Minister for Education and Science v Information Commissioner* [2009] 1 IR 588.

[107] This jurisprudential argument was probably influenced by the New Zealand and Australian freedom of information regimes which have been incorporated in to the interpretation of the Irish rules as previously discussed.

legal opinion. The Attorney General is appointed by the President on the nomination of the Taoiseach. Article 30.3 states that all crimes and offences prosecuted in court other than a court with summary jurisdiction (i.e. District Court) are to be prosecuted in the name of the people and at the suit of the Attorney General or other person authorised by law to act for that purpose. However, since the passage of the Prosecution of Offences Act 1974, the Director of Public Prosecutions acts on behalf of the People in order prosecute criminal offences. The role of the Attorney General is now confined to private law work on behalf of the State. The Attorney General is not a member of Government but does sit at cabinet.

The Attorney General may resign at any time by placing his resignation in the hands of the Taoiseach for submission to the President. The Taoiseach may request the resignation of the Attorney General and if the request is not complied with, then the appointment will be terminated by the President. The Attorney General will retire from office when the Taoiseach resigns but can continue his duties until the successor to the Taoiseach is appointed.

### 5.4.2 Comptroller and Auditor General

Under Art 33 of the Constitution, a Comptroller and Auditor General will be appointed to control spending and audit all money administered by the Oireachtas. He will be appointed by the President on the nomination of the Dáil. He cannot be a member of the Dáil or the Seanad and may not hold any other office or paid job. The Comptroller and Auditor General will report to the Dáil and cannot be removed from office except in the case of stated misbehaviour or incapacity and only with resolutions passed by the Dáil and Seanad calling for their removal. The Taoiseach will then notify the president of such resolutions and send on certified copies from the Chair of the House of the Oireachtas. The President can then remove the Comptroller and Auditor General from office.

## 5.5 Local Government

Local government in Ireland has been a feature of local political life since before the independence of the State. However, the role and function of local government was not recognised on a constitutional level until the 20th Amendment to the Constitution in 1999. At present, local government in Ireland consists of 26 county councils, three city councils and two city and county councils, such as Waterford and

Limerick, where the previously separate city council and county council were merged.[108]

The amendment of the Constitution provided for the constitutional recognition of the role of local government by the insertion of Art 28A. This Article

> "recognises the role of local government in providing a forum for the democratic representation of local communities, in exercising and performing at local level powers and functions conferred by law and in promoting by its initiatives the interests of such communities".

The Article provides for directly-elected local authorities as will be determined by law. Their powers and functions will be determined by law. Elections will be held every five years. Every citizen who is entitled to vote for members of Dáil Éireann will be entitled to vote in local elections. This franchise can be extended by law and was extended to include non-nationals. Casual vacancies are to be filled in accordance with law. The law in this regard allows for members to be co-opted on to a local authority. There are currently 949 elected councillors in Ireland across the city, county and city and county councils.[109]

However, the core responsibility for the administration of local government currently rests with the Department of Housing, Planning and Local Government which co-ordinates the activities of local government across the State. The constitutional recognition of local government is expanded legislatively by the Local Government Act 2001 which is subject to amendment by the Local Government Reform Act 2014. The Law Reform Commission has also produced a Consolidated Act which reflects all legislative provisions that pertain to local government.[110] This Act consolidates all relevant legislation to the activities and functions of local government including local elections, planning and development, sanitary services, and roads amongst others.

---

[108] See the Local Government Act 2001 (Revised), available at http://www.lawreform.ie/_fileupload/RevisedActs/WithAnnotations/HTML/EN_ACT_2001_0037.HTM (accessed 28 November 2017).

[109] See the Local Government Act 2001 (Revised), available at http://www.lawreform.ie/_fileupload/RevisedActs/WithAnnotations/HTML/EN_ACT_2001_0037.HTM (accessed 28 November 2017).

[110] See the Local Government Act 2001 (Revised) http://www.lawreform.ie/_fileupload/RevisedActs/WithAnnotations/HTML/EN_ACT_2001_0037.HTM (accessed 28 November 2017).

# CHAPTER SIX

# THE COURTS AND TRIAL OF OFFENCES

## 6.0 Introduction

The courts are part of the organs of government and form part of the tripartite division of the separation of powers. Their constitutional role will be discussed in this chapter along with the provisions relating to the trial of offences. The constitutional coverage of the courts not only includes the structure of the courts but also the concepts of the administration of justice, access to justice and locus standi. The constitutional provisions relating to the courts are covered in Arts 34 to 37. These articles also include the insertion of a Civil Court of Appeal with the passage of the 33rd Amendment of the Constitution.

Article 34.1 states that:

> "Justice shall be administered in courts established by law by judges appointed in the manner provided by this Constitution, and, save in such special and limited cases as may be prescribed by law, shall be administered in public."

## 6.1 The Courts

### 6.1.1 Structure of the Courts

The provisions of Art 34.2 state that the courts will be comprised of a court of first instance, being the High Court, a court of appeal, being the new Court of Civil Appeal, and a court of final appeal, being the Supreme Court. Under Art 34.4.3°, the Supreme Court will have appellate jurisdiction to the High Court. Since the 33rd Amendment of the Constitution, the Supreme Court can release dissenting judgments on the issue of Constitutional question. The decisions of the Supreme Court are final and conclusive.

The High Court as court of first instance has full original jurisdiction to hear and determine all matters and questions of law or fact whether civil or criminal. The High Court will also have jurisdiction to hear questions relating to the constitutionality of legislation through the procedure of judicial review. Article 34.3 reiterated the rule that no further case will be entertained on a piece of legislation which has survived an Art 26 reference.

Article 34.4 establishes the courts of local and limited jurisdiction which are more commonly referred to as the District and the Circuit Courts.

Article 36 states that issues related to the number of judges, pay, retirement age and pensions, terms of appointment, the constitution and arrangement of the courts including the distribution of business, jurisdiction and matters of procedure are to be regulated by law.

Article 37 deals with the provision of judicial powers to persons or bodies which are not courts such as the Adoption Board, the Master of the High Court and planning authorities.

Article 38 sets out the fundamental constitutional principles which underpin the trial of offences. Article 38.1 states that no person will be tried on any criminal charge save in due course of law. Only minor offences may be tried in courts of summary jurisdiction such as the District Court.

### 6.1.2 Special Courts

Article 38.3.1° allows for the establishment of special courts for the trial of offences where it is determined that the ordinary courts would be unable to secure the effective administration of justice and the preservation of public peace and order. An example of such a court is the Special Criminal Court, where there is no jury as it is believed that such juries could be tampered with and thereby undermine the effective administration of justice. The jurisdiction of such courts will be prescribed by law. Outside of these courts, no person can be tried on a non-minor criminal charge without a jury. The provisions of this Article also provides for the establishment of military tribunals for those subject to military law.

### 6.1.3 Treason

Article 39 states the definition of treason under the Constitution:

> "Treason shall consist only in levying war against the State, or assisting any State or person or inciting or conspiring with any person to levy war against the State, or attempting by force of arms or other violent means to overthrow the organs of government established by this Constitution, or taking part or being concerned in or inciting or conspiring with any person to make or to take part or be concerned in any such attempt."

## 6.2 Independence of the Judiciary

It has been said that "[j]ustice must not only be done, but be seen to be done"[1] and public confidence is an essential party of the maintenance of a legal system which is respected and followed by the general population. Therefore, the Oath of Office states that judges will discharge their duties "without fear or favour, affection or ill-will towards any man".

The oath of all judges appointed under the Constitution is set out under the provisions of Art 34.5.1° as follows:

> "In the presence of Almighty God I do solemnly and sincerely promise and declare that I will duly and faithfully and to the best of my knowledge and power execute the office of Chief Justice (or as the case may be) without fear or favour, affection or ill-will towards any man, and that I will uphold the Constitution and the laws. May God direct and sustain me."

This declaration will be made and subscribed by the Chief Justice in the presence of the President, and by each of the other judges of the Supreme Court, the judges of the High Court and the judges of every other court in the presence of the Chief Justice or the senior available judge of the Supreme Court in open court. The declaration will also be made and subscribed by every judge before entering upon his duties as such judge, and in any case not later than 10 days after the date of his appointment or such later date as may be determined by the President. Any judge who declines or neglects to make this declaration will be deemed to have vacated office.

Article 35.1 states that all judges will be appointed by the President. Article 35.2 establishes that all judges will be independent in the exercise of their powers. No judge can be a member of either House of the Oireachtas and cannot hold any other office or paid employment.

Article 35.5.1° states that the pay of judges cannot be reduced during their continuance in office. However, the pay of judges is subject to taxes and levies placed on other public and civil servants where those deductions are made in the public interest. These provisions were the subject of a judicial pay referendum, as a handful of judges would not voluntarily comply with public sector pension levy payments and higher tax rates during the financial crisis.

 Judges of the Supreme Court and High Court can only be removed for stated misbehaviour or incapacity and only then by resolutions passed by the Dáil and Seanad calling for their removal. The Taoiseach must

---

[1]   *R v Sussex Justices, Ex p McCarthy* [1924] 1 KB 256 at 259, per Hewart LJ.

then inform the President of any such resolutions. The President may then remove the judge from office. These provisions have also been interpreted to apply to other judges since *Curtin v Clerk of the Dáil*.[2]

One of the core principles of the administration of justice in Ireland is that it will be carried out in public unless there are legitimate reasons for it being carried out in private, such as in family law cases or in matters relating to juveniles. This issue was explored in *Irish Times v Ireland*.[3] In this case, the right of a judge to remove reporters from court was challenged. The Circuit Court judge in a drugs case was concerned that there may be inaccurate reporting which the judge feared could lead to the discharge of the jury. The Supreme Court held that the direction of the judge was inconsistent with the justice being administered in public and also infringed free speech guarantees in the Constitution.

## 6.3 Access to Justice

Under the provisions of the Irish Constitution, namely Art 34.1, justice is to be administered in public, and therefore the courts should be accessible to all regardless of their financial position. Also under the Constitution, there is an express right of access to the court and all persons are equal before the law. This impacts on the right to be informed of criminal proceedings and the right of members of the public to attend cases. This right is limited with regard to proceedings held *in camera* such as juvenile justice, family law courts and cases where trade secrets or official information are being discussed e.g. state secrets or intelligence reports in national security cases. The right of access to court for the deprivation of liberty is covered in Art 40.4.2°. This right is further developed in the consideration of the right to fair trial. Other issues arise when the costs of defending or taking a case are at issue. Not every person has the financial means to engage solicitors and barristers to ensure that their legal rights are up held. But as R Byrne and JP McCutcheon phrased it, "[t]he law, like the Ritz Hotel, is open to all".[4] It has long been a tradition of the legal profession to take on what is known as *pro bono* work, work where by the practitioner does not expect to receive any payment for the work. However, not all prospective litigants will have their cases taken on a *pro bono* basis.

As stated above the provisions of Art 40.4 ensure that the punishment of imprisonment is constitutionally sanctioned. Only those that have

---

2   [2006] IESC 14.
3   *The Irish Times v Ireland* [1998] 1 IR 359.
4   R Byrne, JP McCutcheon and C Bruton, *Byrne and McCutcheon on the Irish Legal System* (5th ed, Bloomsbury Professional, Dublin, 2009), p 356.

been tried in accordance with the law of the State as set out by the Constitution may be lawfully deprived of their liberty, liberty being a fundamental human right. The provisions of Art 40.4.2° allow for the testing of the lawfulness of detention in what Byrne and McCutcheon consider to be a "modern version of the *habeus corpus* procedure".[5] Also from this provision, the use of legal professionals such as solicitors and barristers cannot be forced on a prospective applicant. In fact, courts are generally more accommodating to the lay litigant or the litigant *pro se*, to give the formal title. Also, a knowledgeable friend of the lay litigant may be allowed to help them. This person is known as a 'McKenzie friend' which was defined in *McKenzie v McKenzie*[6] as follows:

> "Any persons, whether he be a professional man or not, may attend as a friend of either party, may take notes, may quietly make suggestions, and give advice: but no one can demand to take part in the proceedings as an advocate, contrary to the regulations of the court as settled by the discretion of the justices."[7]

*An amicus curiae* is another person who may assist with access to justice and the courts in complex litigation and is linked to the concept of the McKenzie friend. According to Gray, the translation means a "friend of the tribunal or court" —a person who is not a party to proceedings is permitted to take an active part to assist with research, argument and submissions where one person is not represented or where an independent view is deemed appropriate.[8] Where a young person under the age of 18 is involved in proceedings the court may appoint a guardian *ad litem* if they do not have a parent or guardian to act in their interests. Such a person may also be appointed for those of reduced mental capacity.

Up until 1962, a person would only be granted free legal aid in the case of a criminal charge where he faced the death penalty. Until this time, it was not uncommon for a person facing a serious charge to be represented by a junior counsel only, whereas the State would be represented by a senior counsel and a junior counsel. There was therefore a serious imbalance in proceedings which needed to be addressed.

---

[5]  R Byrne, JP McCutcheon and C Bruton, *Byrne and McCutcheon on the Irish Legal System* (5th ed, Bloomsbury Professional, Dublin, 2009), p 351.
[6]  [1971] P 33. This judgment was essentially a restatement of a similar provision from *Collier v Hicks* (1831) 2 B & Ad 663.
[7]  *Collier v Hicks* (1831) 2 B & Ad 663 at 669.
[8]  J Gray, *Lawyers' Latin–A Vade Mecum* (Robert Hale, London 2002), p 31.

Under the provisions of the Criminal Justice (Legal Aid) Act 1962 (the '1962 Act'), a system of criminal legal aid was provided for. This legal aid would be provided in instances where it appears to the District Court judge or the trial judge that the defendant's means are insufficient to enable them to engage representations from their own resources and that the charge is such or circumstances are exceptional enough to warrant the need for legal aid. This scheme only refers to legal assistance that is assigned by the court, and the solicitors and barristers that work under this scheme opt to represent clients under the 1962 Act. However, where a defendant had nominated a solicitor to represent him, then this request will be granted.

The importance of access to criminal legal aid is highlighted by *The State (Healy) v Donoghue*[9] where the failure to inform an accused of his right to criminal aid, even if a person has pleaded guilty, will violate his constitutional rights. In this case, an accused was facing a number of serious criminal allegations. The accused was 18, almost illiterate and had not been fully informed of his right to legal aid. At the first instance, the accused did not apply for legal aid as he was not informed of it. At a later stage, he then applied for legal aid and representation was granted to him for subsequent hearings. However, his solicitor later withdrew due to disputes regarding the implementation of the 1962 Act. The judicial review was due to the prosecuting solicitor's application for a stay on proceedings for a new solicitor to be appointed to represent the accused under the terms of the 1962 Act being rejected. In the Supreme Court, O'Higgins CJ stated the importance of the operation of the criminal legal aid scheme as follows:

> "No one can be compelled to accept legal aid, and a person charged is entitled to waive his right in this respect and to defend himself … However, if a person who is ignorant of his rights fails to apply and on that account is not given legal aid then, in my view, his constitutional right is violated. For this reason it seems to me that when a person faces a possible prison sentence and has no lawyer, and cannot provide for one, he ought to be informed of his right to legal aid. If the person charged does not know of his right, he cannot exercise it; if he cannot exercise it, his right is violated."[10]

The provision of criminal legal aid highlighted the lack of State support for civil legal aid. The constitutional interpretation at the time focused on the provision of criminal aid due to the provisions of Art 40.4.2°

---

[9] [1976] IR 325.
[10] *ibid* at 325.

which was interpreted to hold for criminal cases only. However, there was growing pressure for the introduction of civil legal aid from both constitutional challenges and advocacy from civil society. The first case to challenge the non-provision of civil legal aid was in *O'Shaughnessy v Attorney General*,[11] where the High Court rejected the argument that the Criminal Justice (Legal Aid) Act 1962 was unconstitutional, as it did not include the provision of civil legal aid. O'Keeffe P stated that the manner in which personal rights of the citizen were to be vindicated were a matter exclusively within the remit of the Oireachtas.

However, the main developments for civil legal aid arose from representations made by Free Legal Aid Centres. From this lobbying, the government set up the Committee on Civil Legal Aid and Advice to make recommendations. The Committee's report[12] recommended that a non-statutory scheme for legal aid be introduced in 1979 with a statutory scheme to follow in the medium term.

In the interim, an application was lodged with the European Court of Human Rights to the effect that the absence of a civil legal aid scheme was in breach of the European Convention on Human Rights (the "ECHR"). According to the provisions of Art 6 of the ECHR

> "In the determination of his civil rights and obligations or of any criminal charge against him, everyone is entitled to a fair and public hearing within a reasonable time by an independent and impartial tribunal established by law. Judgment shall be pronounced publicly but the press and public may be excluded from all or part of the trial in the interests of morals, public order or national security in a democratic society, where the interests of juveniles or the protection of the private life of the parties so require, or to the extent strictly necessary in the opinion of the court in special circumstances where publicity would prejudice the interests of justice."[13]

---

[11] Unreported, High Court, O'Keeffe P, 16 February 1971.
[12] *Report of the Committee on Civil Legal Aid and Advice* (Prl 6862, 1977).
[13] Art 6 of European Convention on Human Rights. It should also be noted that at the time of this application, Ireland was a Convention Member State but the judgments of the ECtHR and principals of the ECHR did not have any domestic effect in Ireland due to the operation of Art 29 of the Constitution. Therefore the Irish government did not have to pay any heed to the judgment and could delay in the reform of Irish law, as in *Norris v Ireland*. The position has since changed with the signing of the Good Friday Agreement, which made the domestic implementation of the ECHR a condition of peace. The European Human Rights Act 2003 now extends the provision of the ECHR to the domestic jurisdiction of Ireland.

The European Court of Human Rights (ECtHR) held that the government's failure to put in place a system of civil legal aid breached Art 6.1.

The first development in the area of free legal aid for civil cases started with the Free Legal Advice Centres, also known as FLAC, in 1969. FLAC was set up by law students who established law centres where members of the public could get legal advice. These centres were staffed on a voluntary basis by the students and practising lawyers made their services available free of charge to help initiate court proceedings. In the wake of the Civil Legal Aid report and the *Airey* judgment, the government implemented a civil non-statutory scheme. The early scheme was widely criticised for being under-funded and the reality of the underfunding meant that the operation of the scheme was mainly confined to family law cases. The non-statutory nature of the scheme also meant that the operation of civil legal aid was not codified in grounding legislation. This was to change in 1995 with the introduction of the Civil Legal Aid Act which placed the scheme on a concrete statutory footing which outlined the nature of the Legal Aid board and its composition, and defined both legal aid[14] and legal advice.[15] The Act also stipulates the tests for eligibility for free legal aid and the means test to be taken. The criteria for receiving legal aid are set down in s 28(2) and the excluded matters are contained in s 28(9). For example, cases concerning defamation, election petitions and test cases are excluded. This is even though there is a constitutional right to a good name and the Legal Aid Board owes its existence to the use of a test case in the first place. It could be argued that this is due to the costs associated with such litigation. For such litigation, prospective plaintiffs have to rely on the benevolence of lawyers to work under *pro bono* schemes. The placing of the Legal Aid Board on a statutory footing has allowed persons who have suffered delays in the processing of their application to seek judicial assistance. In *Kavanagh v Legal Aid Board*,[16] the applicant claimed that a delay of 20 months amounted to a breach of the Legal Aid Board's statutory duty. Butler J dismissed the application, stating that even though there was a statutory duty to provide assistance, this was subject to the Board's resources. However, in *O'Donoghue v Legal Aid Board*, the plaintiff was successful on similar grounds to *Kavanagh*. Here the plaintiff had suffered a delay of 25 months and Kelly J stated that the delay in providing legal aid, even though subject to the Board's resources, amounted to a breach of the applicants right to access the court.

---

14  s 27.
15  s 25.
16  [2001] IEHC 149.

### 6.4 *Locus Standi*

*Locus standi* refers to an ability of a person to take a case on a point of law. Generally *locus standi* will be interpreted narrowly in order to prevent a large number of cases being taken on an issue by those that have not been directly affected. As stated in *Cahill v Sutton*[17] by Henchy J:

> "The primary rule as to standing in constitutional matters is that the person challenging the constitutionality of the statute, or some other person for whom he is deemed by the court to be entitled to speak, must be able to assert that, because of the alleged unconstitutionality, his or that other person's interests have been adversely affected, or stand in real or imminent danger of being adversely affected by the operation of the statute."[18]

However, in constitutional law the rules of standing are somewhat more relaxed where the public at large may be impacted by legislation infringing the provisions of the Constitution. For example, in *Society for the Protection of the Unborn Child v Coogan*,[19] the primary issue in the case was the provisions of information regarding abortion services, which services were available in England, but not in Ireland, as the procedure was repugnant to the Constitution under Art 40.3.3° as constituted at the time of the action.[20] The court allowed the society to bring the action as, even though they were obviously not unborn children that would be affected by the information, they were able to litigate on behalf of the unborn child that is given constitutional protection. In *Crotty v An Taoiseach*,[21] Mr Crotty was able to take a case on the ability of the executive to sign up to EU treaties without putting before the people as part of a referendum. This was allowed as an *actio popularis* to protect the rights of the public as a whole. With the introduction of a more relaxed approach for constitutional issues, a balance has to be achieved between allowing for all valid cases to be subject to review, but also managing to avert vexatious litigants. An example would be in *Riordan v Ireland (No.4)*[22] where a litigant with a long history of taking cases was ordered to apply for leave from the court for further cases to act as a filter on his challenges while still maintaining access to justice.

---

[17] [1980] IR 269.
[18] *Cahill v Sutton* [1980] IR 269 at 286.
[19] [1989] IR 734.
[20] See now the Protection of Life During Pregnancy Act 2013.
[21] [1987] IR 713.
[22] [2001] 3 IR 365.

Sem 2 -

## 6.5 Trial of Offences

The Constitution sets out protections for fair trials in a number of different Articles in the Constitution which are grouped here for consideration. The Constitution references these right in terms of the concept of "in due course of law". In general, the Constitution reaffirms rights to fair trial and treatment of suspects that were already well established in the common law system, such as the right to a trial by jury. However, as the Constitution forms a contract between the citizens and the State for its administration it is essential that these are set out in the Constitution in a way that guarantees the application of these rights but in a manner that is flexible, to ensure due process and interpretation in cases without being overly prescriptive which may, an unintended consequence, fetter the provision of such rights. In general, constitutional issues should be raised only when all matters of criminal procedure have been exhausted. Humphreys J in *Bita v DPP*[23] stated that the principle of "reaching constitutional issues last" means that an applicant should "generally exhaust his or her remedies in the criminal process before bringing an application for judicial review".

Article 38.1 states that "no person will be tried on any criminal charge save in due course of law".[24] As the Constitution does not state what is meant by the phrase "due course of law", it has been left to judicial interpretation to flesh out what is meant by this phrase. This has been done by interpreting the provisions of the Constitution and looking at common law norms that have been developed to ensure fair trials and to uphold constitutional justice. A person has a right to liberty under the provisions of Art 40.4.1°, which states that "no citizen shall be deprived of his personal liberty save in accordance with law". For this reason, the Constitution clearly outlines the habeas corpus provisions to challenge the detention of an individual.[25] Even where a person has been imprisoned, certain fundamental rights still continue to be enjoyed such as the right to life as there is no capital punishment in Ireland[26], the right to vote and the right to communicate. Any infringement of these rights when an individual is imprisoned may also invalidate their detention. The phrase "due course of law" was considered by Gannon J. in *State (Healy) v Donoghue*[27] as follows:

> "A phrase of very wide import which includes in its scope not merely matters of constitutional and statutory jurisdiction, the range of legislation with respect to criminal

---

23  [2016] IEHC 288.
24  Art 38.1.
25  Art 40.4.1° to Art 40.4.4°.
26  See the consideration of the right to life in section 7.5.
27  [1976] IR 325.

offences, and matters of practice and procedure, but also the application of basic principles of justice which are inherent in the proper course of the exercise of the judicial function."[28]

Any individual who is subject to criminal law proceedings is to be presumed innocent until proven guilty. In *King v Attorney General*,[29] the provision relating to loitering with intent was found to be unconstitutional as it presupposed criminal intent on behalf of the person that was subject to the charge. For these reasons, there are specific protections for suspects which include bail, a fair trial, rights on arrest and during detention, and a right to silence. The presumption of innocence has been described in the following terms by Walsh J in *People (Attorney General) v O'Callaghan*[30] as "a very real thing and not simply a procedural rule taking effect only at trial".[31] It was further described by Murray J in *POC v DPP*[32] as:

> "personal to the dignity and status of every citizen. It means that he or she is entitled to the status of a person innocent of criminal charges until such as been proven in a court conducted in accordance with law."[33]

### 6.5.1 Arrest and Detention

When an individual is arrested in connection with an alleged offence, he must be charged with a crime. A person must be charged with an offence that is known to the law, as per *Attorney General v Cunningham*.[34] This is a fundamental element of Irish criminal law, constitutional law and common law, and is a protection against arbitrary prosecutions. It was also established in *People (Attorney General) v Edge*.[35] Suspects also have the right to be informed of their right to remain silent.[36] There should be sufficient time given for an accused to prepare their defence.[37]

It is not permissible for a person to be held for questioning. Arrest is not to be made for the purposes of questioning. An arrest is only to be

---

[28]  *ibid* at 335.
[29]  [1981] IR 233.
[30]  [1966] IR 501.
[31]  *The People (Attorney General) v O'Callaghan* [1966] IR 501 at 513.
[32]  [2003] 3 IR 87.
[33]  *POC v DPP* [2003] 3 IR 87 at 103.
[34]  [1932] IR 28.
[35]  [1943] IR 115.
[36]  A full discussion of this right will take place further on in this section.
[37]  *O'Callaghan v Clifford* [1993] 3 IR 603.

made to charge someone with a crime. In *People (DPP) v O'Loughlin*,[38] the defendant voluntarily went to a Garda station to answer questions about one issue. However, without being charged, he was taken to a different Garda station and questioned about a separate issue. While under questioning, he made an incriminating statement. The Court of Appeal held that this was a deliberate violation of the individual's rights. In *People (DPP) v Coffey*,[39] the accused was not informed that he was free to leave and it found that his detention was unlawful. However, in appropriately serious cases once the questioning is proportionate and justified by the public interest in combating serious crime, it may be deemed to be constitutional, as in *People (DPP) v Quilligan (No.1)*.[40] Under *State (Trimbole) v Governor of Mountjoy Prison*,[41] Egan J specifically stated that the courts were under a duty to protect individuals against the invasion of an individual's constitution rights as follows:

> "Courts have no higher duty to perform than that involving the protection of constitutional rights and if at any time the protection of those rights should delay, or even defeat, the ends of justice in a particular case, it is better for the public good that this should happen rather than that constitutional rights should be nullified."[42]

The general rule is that an accused should be charged as soon as possible within the statutorily permissible timeframes. For example, under s 30 of the Offences against the State Act 1939, which mainly deals with terrorism-related offences, there are scheduled offences where an accused can be arrested and held for up to 24 hours, which may be extended by another 24 hours. Since the Offences against the State (Amendment Act) 1989, this period can be extended for a further 24 hour period with leave of the district court which amounts to a total permissible period of detention for up to three days.

Under s 4 of the Criminal Justice Act 1984, any person arrested for an offence that is punishable by more than five years in prison or more can be detained for an initial six hour period and this may be extended to a full 24 hour period. The Criminal Justice (Drug Trafficking) Act 1996 can allow for a total possible period of arrest for up to seven days with extensions, and arrest under s 50 of the Criminal Justice Act 2007

---

38  [1979] IR 85.
39  [1987] ILRM 727.
40  [1986] IR 49.
41  [1985] IR 550.
42  *ibid* at 565.

can result in up to a seven-day period of detention for serious offences involving firearms and explosives.

While in detention, Garda questioning cannot be oppressive.[43] There is a legal duty imposed on Gardaí to inform an accused that there is a right to consult a solicitor.[44] It is also not permitted to exhaust a confession out of an accused.[45] Nor is it permitted to take a confession from an individual while he is under the influence of drugs, controlled substances or hypnosis.[46]

### 6.5.2 Right to Bail

Bail is usually granted between arrest and trial. The right to bail goes hand in hand with the presumption of innocence, as no person may be deprived of their liberty until they have been found guilty following a trial in due course of law. Bail is granted upon the condition that the accused will return to court for his trial, and a bond is placed with the court which will be forfeited if they do not return for trial. There may be other conditions imposed by the court, such as signing on at a Garda station or handing in one's passport. Prior to the 1997 referendum, bail could only be refused if it was likely that the accused would 'skip bail', intimidate witnesses or interfere with evidence. Prior to the amendment of the provisions, the court could not refuse bail on the grounds that the accused would re-offend as this would presupposed that the suspect was guilty; see *People (Attorney General) v O'Callaghan*[47] and *Ryan v DPP*.[48]

Since the 1997 referendum and insertion of Art 40.4.6° into the Constitution, bail may now be refused by a court to a person who is "charged with a serious offence where it is reasonably considered necessary to prevent the commission of a serious offence by that person". Bail for murder cases is now dealt with by the High Court.[49] The Bail Act 1997 was introduced following the referendum to flesh out the new provisions. This Act includes a schedule of offences to be considered as serious offences such as murder, rape and certain offences including firearms and explosives, and any offence that may be punished by more than five years. The court must also consider issues such as the degree of seriousness of the offence, the strength

---

[43] *People (DPP) v Madden* [1977] IR 336.
[44] Under both s 5 of the Criminal Justice Act 1984 and *People (DPP) v Healy* [1990] ILRM 313.
[45] *People (DPP) v McNally* (1981) 2 Frewen 43.
[46] *People (DPP) v Shaw* [1982] IR 1.
[47] [1966] IR 501.
[48] [1989] IR 399.
[49] *ibid.*

of evidence against the defendant, the likely sentence to be given if convicted, any previous convictions especially crimes committed while on bail, whether the accused has or may have a drug addiction and the likelihood that the accused will commit a crime while on bail.

### 6.5.3 Rights at Trial

There is no express right in the Constitution to an early trial. However, a right to an early trial, or one without excessive delay, was found to be a constitutional right in *State (O'Connell) v Fawsitt*.[50] The US decision in *Barker v Wingo* on the issue of an early trial has been cited in a number of Irish cases[51] as follows in terms of the prejudice that might affect the accused when there is no early trial:

> "Prejudice should be assessed in the light of the interest of defendants which the speedy trial right was designed to protect. This court has identified three such interests:
> To prevent oppressive pretrial incarceration;
> To minimise anxiety and concern of the accused; and
> To limit the possibility that the defence will be impaired."[52]

In *State (O'Connell) v Fawsitt*,[53] the court interpreted this right in terms of Art 38.1 explicitly guaranteeing the right to trial with reasonable expedition. In *NC v DPP*,[54] there was a nine year delay in raising a complaint of sexual abuse which was deemed to have affected the accused's right to a trial with reasonable expedition. Barr J held that this delay was "unreasonably long in all the circumstances".[55] Even though in criminal law there is no statute of limitations or time limit in which to commence an action, where there is a delay in commencing proceedings, there may be concerns with regard to issues such as witness evidence. There is no time bar on bringing actions and the court may still hear such cases, but where the delay has been so excessive that it could be considered to be prejudicial, this may represent an interference with the accused's constitutional rights.[56] There are many reasons why there may be a delay in criminal charges, such as historic

---

[50] [1986] IR 362.
[51] *DPP v Byrne* [1994] 2 IR 236, *PC v DPP* [1999] 1 IR 25 to mention a few.
[52] *Barker v Wingo* 407 US 514 (1972) at 532.
[53] [1986] IR 362.
[54] [1991] 1 IR 471.
[55] *ibid* at 475. However, Hogan and Whyte add that it must be remembered that this comment was made before the "torrent of sexual abuse cases" that came before the courts: G Hogan and G Whyte, *JM Kelly: The Irish Constitution* (4th ed, Tottel Publishing, Dublin, 2006), p 1115.
[56] *H v DPP* [2006] IESC 55.

child sex abuse allegations, but the right to a fair trial will be the main concern as in *B v DPP*.[57]

Article 15.5.1° prohibits the creation of retrospective law, and therefore the charge must be one which was known to the law at the time the offence was committed.[58] The charge must be laid in the presence of a judge. Normally this is carried out in at a sitting of the District Court. Where the charge is to be laid outside of normal sitting times, there will generally be a special sitting of the District Court area in which the offence took place at the earliest possible time. An individual has a number of rights in this instance: they have the right to be informed of the charges,[59] a right to have access to, and consult with a solicitor,[60] and access to free criminal legal aid where required.[61]

An individual has a right to be present at his trial as established in *The People (Attorney General) v Messitt*.[62] However, once the essentials of constitutional justice are observed, there is no absolute rule that his must be present for his trial[63]; in *People (Director of Public Prosecutions) v Kelly*,[64] a trial was held in the absence of the accused had absconded. An accused has a right to be informed of the charges against him.[65] An accused has the right to defend himself against the charges brought against him and to conduct a cross-examination.[66] This right also extended to the provision of criminal legal aid, as in *State (Healy) v Donoghue*,[67] which consequently allows for a defendant to prepare and present a defence through his legal counsel. The defendant also has a right to understand proceedings, as was held in *State (Buchan) v Coyne*[68] where the defendant was not an Irish speaker and the District Court judge did not allow for Garda evidence given in Irish to be translated in order for the defendant to make his case. An accused has the right

---

57 [1997] ILRM 118.
58 See *Enright v Ireland* [2003] 2 IR 321. This is also reflected in Art 7 European Convention of Human Rights.
59 *People (DPP) v Walsh* [1980] IR 29.
60 *People (DPP) v Healy* [1990] ILRM 313.
61 *State (Healy) v Donoghue* [1976] IR 325 and see section 6.3 on access to justice.
62 [1974] IR 204.
63 This is evident from the provisions of s 50(4A) b of the Criminal Justice Act 2007 as amended by s 23 of the Criminal Justice Act 2009 even the accused, their legal representatives and the media do not have an automatic right to be present in court for any hearing to extend periods of detention where the presence of these individuals may prejudice an on-going investigation
64 [1982] IR 1.
65 *State (Howard) v Donnelly* [1966] IR 51 and *Berine v Garda Commissioner* [1993] ILRM 1.
66 *Gill v Connellan* [1987] IR 541 and also see *State (Walshe) v Murphy* [1981] IR 275.
67 [1976] IR 325.
68 (1936) 70 ILTR 185.

to cross-examine but not necessarily confront their accuser. This point was made in *Donnelly v Ireland*,[69] where the use of video-link evidence was questioned. Under the Criminal Evidence Act 1992, a child alleged to be the victim of sexual abuse could give evidence via video-link and the constitutionality of this provision was upheld by the court as the right to cross-examine was maintained.

The question and approach of the courts towards the use of unconstitutionally obtained evidence has changed of recent in the case of *DPP v JC*.[70] The previous statement of the law on this point was that it was not possible for unconstitutionally obtained evidence to be used in court—for example, information obtained from a home without a warrant. Where there was an accidental breach as in the case of *People (AG) v O'Brien*,[71] evidence would be allowed if there was no deliberate breach of rights. Since the *JC*[72] case, the position has changed with regard to extraordinary excusing circumstances where the circumstances surrounding collection of the unconstitutionally obtained evidence would excuse the breach. The current position is that inadvertent breaches of constitutional right in the collection of evidence for prosecution will not automatically lead to the evidence being excluded. However, if such evidence is knowingly, recklessly or negligently collected in violation of an individual's rights, then such material will be excluded unless there are exceptional circumstances in the case to require such evidence to be entered at trial.

An individual's sentence must be pronounced in court. In *State (Kiernan) v deBúrca*,[73] it was stated that it is a "fundamental rule that the pronouncement of a sentence following a conviction was an essential part of the administration of justice in the case".[74] There is a right to a certain and proportionate sentence where there is a definite beginning and end to the term of imprisonment and it must not be arbitrary or disproportionate, as stated in *Cox v Ireland*.[75] Another example of disproportionate penalties is in the case of *Lovett v Minister for Education*,[76] where the right to a State pension for a teacher was nullified if an individual was sentenced to a period of imprisonment of more than 12 months.

The rule against double jeopardy, which is sometimes referred to

---

[69]  [1998] 1 IR 325.
[70]  [2015] IESC 31.
[71]  [1965] IR 142.
[72]  [2015] IESC 31.
[73]  [1963] IR 348.
[74]  *ibid* at 366 and has been restated in [1978] IR 438.
[75]  [1992] 2 IR 501.
[76]  [1997] ILRM 89.

as *autrefois acquit*, means that a person cannot be tried again for an offence which they have already been tried for in due course of law. O'Higgins CJ in *People (DPP) v O'Shea*,[77] cited the principle as stated by Blackstone

> "When a man is once fairly found not guilty upon any indictment, or other prosecution, before any court having competent jurisdiction of the offence he may plead such acquittal in bar of any subsequent accusation for the same crime."[78]

This rule was constitutionally confirmed in the case of *People (Director of Public Prosecutions) v Quilligan*.[79] The case concerned a directed acquittal of the defendant in the Central Criminal court and the Supreme Court had to assess whether it had the power to order a re-trial. The court held by a majority that it did not, and two judges in the majority even said that the court had no power to even make such an order as follows

> "The rule of autrefois acquit means that if an accused duly and successfully raised the plea that he has already been tried in a court of competent jurisdiction, action within jurisdiction, for the offence now charged, and that he was acquitted for that charge in that court, for the second trial for that offence may not take place. This rule ... which is sometimes referred to as the rule against double jeopardy, is but an aspect of the canon of fundamental fairness of legal procedures inherent in our Constitution."[80]

However, the concerns raised in the rule against double jeopardy do not apply to appeal cases as in *People (DPP) v O'Shea*.[81]

### 6.5.4 Right to Silence

The right to silence is a fundamental tenet of fair procedures in criminal trials and also a central element of a trial in due course of law. The right to silence is found in the privilege against self-incrimination in the rules of evidence and is also reflected in other common law jurisdictions, such as in the US where the Fifth Amendment of the US Constitution is considered the parallel protection against self-incrimination.[82] A

---

[77]   [1982] IR 384.
[78]   *ibid* at 406.
[79]   [1986] IR 49.
[80]   *ibid* at 57.
[81]   [1982] IR 384.
[82]   This point was made by McCarthy J in *Goodman International v Hamilton (No.1)*

person does not have to incriminate himself and therefore cannot be forced to answer questions put to him, as it is the role of the prosecution to prove the guilt of the defendant rather than the role of the defence to prove that the accused did not commit the crime.

In *Sweeney v Ireland*,[83] the right to silence was considered in connection with the constitutionality of s 4 of the Criminal Justice Act 1984 regarding the provisions concerning the withholding of information from Gardai in connection with a serious crime. In the judgment, Baker J referred to two seminal cases on the point. Mustill LJ in *R v Director of Serious Fraud Office Ex p Smith* stated:

> "… there is the instinct that it is contrary to fair play to put the accused in a position where he is exposed to punishment whatever he does. If he answers, he may condemn himself out of his own mouth; if he refuses he may be punished for his refusal …".[84]

Baker J also referred to the judgment of Barrington J in *Re National Irish Bank Ltd. (No.1)*[85] where the historical and philosophical source of the right to silence and the principle against self-incrimination were discussed as follows:

> "It grew out of the revulsion of the judges for forced confessions as being both unjust in their origin and unreliable in practice. Some judges also seemed to have felt that it was unfair to place a man in a position where he was condemned no matter what he did."

In *Heaney v Ireland*,[86] the right to silence was considered a constitutional right as a corollary to the right to free expression as contained in Art 40.6.1° (i) of the fundamental rights but, as with all constitutional rights, this is not absolute and must be balanced with all other constitutional rights.

## 6.6 Trial by Jury

Under the provisions of Art 38.5, no person shall be tried on any criminal charge without a jury unless it is a minor offence tried by

---

[1992] 2 IR 542.
[83] [2017] IEHC 702.
[84] [1993] AC 1 at 32.
[85] [1999] 3 IR 145 at 177.
[86] [1994] 3 IR 593.

a court of summary jurisdiction,[87] tried by a special court,[88] or by a military tribunal.[89] Hogan and Whyte state that the right to trial by jury is a constitutional imperative and not a personal right.[90] In *Melling v Ó Mathghamhna*,[91] Ó Dálaigh J encapsulated the importance of the trial by jury in the Irish Constitution in the following terms

> "Members (of the jury) are wholly independent of executive or legislative disciplines or displeasure and who necessarily by their very numbers bring to the administration of justice the commoner touch. The safeguard of a trial by jury is against an improbable but not-to-be-overlooked future; and it is for this reason the Constitution enshrines it."[92]

The jury must be representative of the general population. In *de Búrca v Attorney General*,[93] the constitutional guarantee of equality was invoked to ensure female representation on jury panels. Prior to the *de Búrca* case, property-owning men were automatically selected, whereas women had to apply to join a jury panel. This was found to be in contravention of the equality provisions in the Constitution, and did not allow for the formation of juries that were as representative as practical of society. Juries must also be independent and impartial.[94] Forde and Leonard also give the example of the trial of the former Taoiseach Charles Haughey for obstructing the work of the McCracken Tribunal, where the trial judge used a questionnaire for the jury panel to ensure that the selected jurors had not been affected by the pre-trial publicity and issues raised in both the McCracken Tribunal and the Flood Tribunal pertaining to Charles Haughey.[95]

Juries normally comprise of 12 members but where the duration of a trial is likely to exceed 18 months the number may be increased to 15 in order to ensure a sufficient number of jurors.[96]

---

[87]  Art 38.2.

[88]  Art 38.3.

[89]  Art 38.4.

[90]  G Hogan and G Whyte, *JM Kelly: The Irish Constitution* (4th ed, Tottel Publishing, Dublin, 2006), p 1221.

[91]  [1962] IR 1.

[92]  *ibid* at 39.

[93]  [1976] IR 38 also see the consideration of equality in the later chapter.

[94]  See *People (Attorney General) v Singer* [1975] IR 408 which relates to the maxim of *nemo iudex in causa sua*, meaning one cannot be a judge in their own case, which is a fundamental tenet of constitutional justice that there cannot be any bias, whether actual or perceived, on the part of the decision maker.

[95]  M Forde and D Leonard, *Constitutional Law of Ireland* (3rd ed, Bloomsbury Professional, Dublin, 2013), p 480.

[96]  s 15 of the Juries Act 1976 as inserted by s 23 of the Courts and Civil Law (Miscellaneous Provisions) Act 2013.

# CHAPTER SEVEN

# FUNDAMENTAL RIGHTS AND THE CONSTITUTION

## 7.0 Introduction

The purpose of the Constitution is not only to be the foundation document of the structures of State governance, it also contains the fundamental rights guaranteed to the citizens. In a way, it adheres to the idea of a constitution being a form of a social contract between the State and the citizens, by devolving the powers of government to the organs of State in return for guaranteed rights to the citizen.

These rights include, amongst others, the major civil and political rights, the right to family and the right to live and, more recently, children's rights. The personal rights of the citizen are set out in Art 40. This Article sets out the right to equality, the vindication of the personal rights of the citizen, the right to life, good name and property rights of the citizen, the right to personal liberty, inviolability of the dwelling, freedom of expression, the right to assemble, and the freedom to form associations and unions.

The incorporation of these rights has emanated from a literal interpretation of the text and some of the rights have been interpreted into the Constitution by the open nature of some of these rights.[1] For example, the unenumerated rights Article (Art 40.3) has allowed for many rights to be included that may not have been in the contemplation of the framers of the Constitution. This has allowed for the fundamental rights to stay current and reflect changing social influences in the ever-developing State.

Other rights have been brought into the Constitution by means of referendum. These rights did not form part of the rights at the time of the promulgation of the Constitution, but have since been voted in by popular ballot measure, such as the right to divorce, the right to life of the unborn child and children's rights. The process for amending the Constitution is set out in the Constitution itself in Art 46 and the referendum process is set out in Art 47.

## 7.1 Human Rights and the Constitution

The human rights guarantees form a major part of the overall Constitution. It is important to note that all legislation has to follow the Constitution. Therefore, any provisions of legislation which are contrary to the rights of the citizen will be declared unconstitutional and will have no legal effect. The majority of the rights found in this section of the Constitution have parallels in both the European Convention on Human Rights and international human rights

---

[1]   For the process of constitutional interpretation, see section 8.2.

documents, such as the UN Declaration of Human Rights and the International Covenant on Civil and Political Rights. In some cases, the Irish Constitution goes further than these documents, while in others it does not go as far.

The applicability of such documents depends on the degree of incorporation into the Irish domestic legal landscape. Under the provisions of Art 29,[2] the State is entitled to sign such declarations, but they only affect domestic legal provisions if they are incorporated by either referendum or legislation. This means that Ireland is a dualist State with regards to the incorporation of international law.

The European Convention is now part of domestic legislation since the passage of the European Convention on Human Rights Act 2003. However, if a right in the Convention is found to have been infringed by a piece of legislation, then the courts may grant a declaration of incompatibility; however, this has no effect on the continuation of the offending statute. By contrast, documents such as the UN Declaration of Human Rights and the International Covenant on Civil and Political Rights have no domestic effect and do not have to be considered by the Irish courts. An aggrieved citizen may apply to the international tribunals set up under these systems, but their judgments do not have to be recognised by the State.

## 7.2 Absolute Rights and Proportionality

Rights in the Constitution are always based on balancing each right against other competing rights in the Constitution. There are no absolute rights in the Constitution. All rights are subject to limitations and qualifications. For example, the right to political expression under Art 40.6.1(i) allows for the freedom to express convictions and opinions; however, these are subject to public order and restrictions. Under Art 40.3.2°, a person has a right to a reputation, so those exercising their 40.6.1°(i) to speech must also be mindful of defamation provisions. Such absolute issues are also found in other Constitutions and international human rights documents. The only right in the European Convention on Human Rights which is not qualified is the freedom from torture, as it is never considered necessary to torture an individual. Often rights which seem, on their face, to be absolute nonetheless come with related restrictions in their interpretation. The famous US First Amendment right to speech can be restricted. Even though the right states that the US legislature is prohibited from restricting speech, case law demonstrates that the right can

---

[2] For a further discussion of international relations, see section 3.3.

be restricted but the court will look at it closely[3] to ensure that the restriction is reasonable to the aim pursued in the legislation.

This also relates to the principle of proportionality, in that the restriction placed on a right must be proportional to the aims and need for restriction. The idea of proportionality comes from the judicial review of legislation which is claimed to be unconstitutional.[4] In this process, an applicant will have to show that the legislation complained of infringes their constitutional rights to a degree that is not proportionate with the objective of the legislation. This idea of proportionality is also used in the European Court of Human Rights and is developing in the United Kingdom. In *Holland v Governor of Portlaoise Prison*,[5] a ban was put in place to prevent prisoners from communicating with the media. The plaintiff claimed to be wrongly convicted and wished to seek public support for his campaign via the media. There may be legitimate reasons for such a ban yet McKechnie J held that the scope of the restriction went beyond the degree of harm that could be caused by contact with the media and therefore, went beyond what was permissible as a restriction to the plaintiff's right to freedom of expression. This case is a good example of a restriction on a right, in this case freedom of expression, went beyond what would be considered proportionate. The judge held that restrictions only for the purpose of safeguarding security and good order was permissible. Therefore, the ban was unconstitutional. McKechnie J, as an aside, stated that a more balanced approach was to consider each request for contact on its merits.[6]

## 7.3 Personal and Unenumerated Rights

The particular focus of this section will be on the provisions of Article 40.3.1° which states that:

> "The State guarantees in its laws to respect, and, as far as practicable, by its laws to defend and vindicate the personal rights of the citizen."

In this instance, the personal rights of the citizen at the heart of this article are not stated. For this reason, they are known as the unenumerated rights. It is left to the court to interpret what would be considered to be the personal rights of the citizen in this regard.

---

[3]   In a process referred to as "strict scrutiny".
[4]   See section 5.2.3 on the legislative process.
[5]   [2004] 2 IR 573.
[6]   However, this in itself would have to be done with care so as to preserve the right to privacy of an inmate.

Such judicial interpretation of rights has always been controversial. In essence, a set of principles were enshrined as the primary legal source, and yet there is flexibility written into the document. Some may argue that such rights should only be read in accordance to what was in the mind of the framers of the Constitution. However, such provisions are argued to keep constitutional documents relevant to the social conditions in which it operates. This is the case in Ireland.

### 7.3.1 Recognition of Unenumerated Rights

The first case to recognise the existence of implied rights in the Constitution through Art 40.3.1° was *Ryan v Attorney General*.[7] This case is also referred to as the water fluoridation case as the applicant sought to stop the State from putting fluoride in the water without her consent, as she believed that it was detrimental to her health. Even though the applicant was unsuccessful in the totality of her application because she failed to prove the health impacts of fluoride to the court's satisfaction, she was successful in arguing for the right to bodily integrity. This right is not mentioned explicitly in the Constitution, but the judges in the case were able to interpret such as a right as one of the personal rights of the citizen. In the case, Kenny J stated that the use of the words "in particular" in Art 40.3.2° was to create an open list of rights which used the preceding rights as examples of what should be considered instead of the closed list which only recognised those particular rights.

### 7.3.2 Natural Rights or Implied Rights?

Using such a means of interpretation of rights is always controversial, as it is up to the judges to decide from argument what should be considered part of the personal rights and what should not be. It also means that the courts have to tread carefully to ensure that they do not go beyond their remit as arbitrators and become law-makers. In essence, the Constitution is a democratic contract between the citizens and the government whereby powers are granted to the organs of government to delegate the everyday running of democracy to a selected group of people in return for stated rights which will be protected by the State. This contract has been agreed upon by the majority through popular vote, and such rights will only be amended in accordance with popular vote. Therefore, the judiciary must have recourse to the guiding principles and harmonious interpretation of the Constitution in seeking what is permissible. In this respect, it has to be deduced whether such rights are implied from the surrounding document or whether they come from the natural law traditions of the Constitution.

---

[7]   [1965] IR 294.

Natural law can be described as legal rights which exist because of the nature of humanity. In a way, they are regarded as law which is superior to all other forms as it comes from a duty to respect others. This is quite clear with the Preamble's invocation of God and the framing of a number of rights as inalienable, imprescriptible, antecedent and superior to positive law. The opposite to natural law is positive law, where the letter of the law is the most powerful source of law. This philosophy is rejected by the Irish Constitutional structures due to the phrase "antecedent and superior to positive law" in both Arts 41 and 43 dealing with family rights and property respectively.

In *Ryan v Attorney General*,[8] Kenny J suggested that unenumerated rights arose from the "Christian and democratic nature of the State". This test was cited with approval in *Kennedy v Ireland*,[9] where the right to privacy was found to be a natural right which was inherent in the individual by virtue of their human personality.

Implied rights can also be found in the Constitution. They are, in the main, the corollary to an express right. For example, if one has the right to communicate, then one has a right to silence. The existence of an express right to do something also allows for the exercise of the right not to do something. This can be seen in the right to association and unions. You have the right to join a union if you wish to do so, but you also have the opposite right not to join a union if you want, as in *Educational Company v Fitzpatrick (No. 2)*.[10]

We have already seen the right to bodily integrity at the start of this section. The number and scope of the unenumerated rights being recognised by the court is ever-expanding and covers issues from immigration to fair procedures. The list of unenumerated rights is being constantly expanded, not by judicial law-making, but by interpreting what is in line with the tenor of the constitutional document and therefore, what could be considered to be the other personal rights of the citizen that were not expressly written down in the document. For example, the most recent right to be considered by the court and included as part of the unenumerated rights doctrine is the right to the environment as in *Merriman v Fingal County Council*,[11] where Barrett J held:

> "A right to an environment that is consistent with the human dignity and well-being of citizens at large is an essential

---

[8]   [1965] IR 294.
[9]   [1987] IR 587.
[10]  [1961] IR 135.
[11]  [2017] IEHC 695.

condition for the fulfilment of all human rights. It is an indispensable existential right that is enjoyed universally, yet which is vested personally as a right that presents and can be seen always to have presented, and to enjoy protection, under Art. 40.3.1° of the Constitution."[12]

### 7.3.3 The Development of Unenumerated Rights

There are a large number of unenumerated rights which have been recognised by judicial interpretation of Art 40.3.1°. In order to demonstrate how they have come about and the issues that are relevant to their creation, the right to communicate and the right to privacy are discussed in detail here as examples.

#### 7.3.3.1 The Right to Privacy

This right originated from the *McGee v Attorney General*.[13] In this case, a married couple were prevented from accessing contraception. They claimed that their marital privacy was invaded when an illegal consignment was stopped by customs. At the time, the sale and supply of contraceptives was illegal. Mrs McGee was told that she would be putting her life in jeopardy if she were to become pregnant again. The court ruled that this prohibition infringed the privacy of a married couple. This right to privacy was then developed from a completely different angle in the case of *Kennedy v Ireland*.[14] This time the unlawful wiretap of journalists' phones was to broaden the unenumerated right from the confines of marriage to the receipt of communications.[15] The home phones of two political correspondents, Geraldine Kennedy and Bruce Arnold, were tapped without authorisation by the then Minister for Justice. The phone tapping was carried out as the cabinet believed that there was a 'mole' within government which was divulging State secrets to these particular journalists. They wished to discover the identity of the informant.

Even though the Supreme Court held that the protection of State secrets was a justified and legitimate aim, the actions of the government were not proportionate. The court held that the unauthorised interference amounted to a "deliberate, conscious and unjustified intrusion by the servants of the State" to protect executive secrecy indirectly resulted

---

[12] *ibid*, at para 264.

[13] [1974] IR 284.

[14] [1987] IR 587.

[15] See J Kavanagh, "Executive Secrecy and Access to Policy: Lessons from the Past in Irish Legal and Political History" (2012) No. 7, *Working Papers in History and Policy*, available at https://papers.ssrn.com/sol3/papers.cfm?abstract_id=2279027 (accessed 9 February 2018).

in demonstrating the unenumerated right to privacy as part of the personal rights of the citizen.[16] Moreover, the action was

> "without any lawful justification ... [and] constituted an attack on their dignity and freedom as individuals and journalists and cannot be tolerated in a democratic society such as ours ... [and] has been done by an organ of the state which is under a constitutional obligation to respect, vindicate and defend their rights".[17]

### 7.3.3.2 The Right to Communicate

The right to communicate emanated from a case where An Post's communications monopoly on postal services was challenged by a private courier firm. In *Attorney General v Paperlink*,[18] the right to communicate in a general liberal sense was created.

The ability to expand Art 40.3.1° to encompass a secondary right to freedom of expression was probably an unintended consequence of having both a general right to "defend and vindicate the personal rights of the citizen" and a right to express convictions and opinions. A lacuna between the two was filled by the judgment in *Paperlink* which focused on the expansion of Art 40.3 in relation to the liberal speech rights. This case was the first to establish that there was a general right to communicate in the Constitution which was separate to the right to express convictions and opinions as found in Art 40.6.1°. This so-called "liberal speech right" was to later create a tension when both articles were invoked in the protection of political speech.

The key jurisprudential argument is that the role of the political speech protections encompassed by Art 40.6.1° does allow for a lacuna whereby convictions and opinions may be protected if they do not fall foul of the restrictions in Art 40.6.1°, but the right to pure expression itself needs constitutional protection. This is best served under the provisions of Art 40.3.1° where it is given its true home as a personal right of a citizen. Whether this was due to an oversight by the original drafters or a clause that was so obvious that it was without need for enumeration is not known, but its incorporation by means of judicial review only strengths the protection for freedom of expression in the Irish constitutional framework.

However, the development of this right was to cloud the waters in

---

[16]   [1987] IR 587 at 594.
[17]   *ibid* at 594.
[18]   [1984] ILRM 373.

the differentiation between the boundaries of the political right to communicate as incorporated in Art 40.6.1° (i) and the beginnings of this "liberal" right to communicate.

## 7.4 Equality

Article 40.3.1° is the constitutional guarantee of equality. However, the exercise of this right can be restricted by the State as it must pay "due regard to differences of capacity, physical and moral, and of social functions". This is the first example of restrictions on rights in the Constitution in this section. Therefore, this means that even though the idea of constitutional justice is to hold all equal and distribute rights equally, the State is able to discriminate legitimately under the terms of the Constitution. So, for example, the provision of extra teaching staff to a special needs student does not discriminate against another student as the teaching allocation is based on the needs of the students. Also, the provision of maternity leave to female staff is not breaching equality for male workers.

In practice, this constitutional guarantee has proven weak in the majority of cases, but it has proven useful in cases of gender inequality and equality in the political process. In *de Burca v Attorney General*,[19] the Juries Act 1927 was held to be unconstitutional as only men were required to serve on juries. The role of equality is also gaining favour in relation to political speech cases. In *McKenna v An Taoiseach (No.2)*,[20] three of the judges highlighted that there must be equality in access to the media on referendum issues and that allocation of government funds to lobby for one result over another was unconstitutional. However, this did not mean that the result of the divorce referendum was null and void.[21] The *McKenna* case led to the establishment of the Referendum Commission to raise awareness of the holding of a referendum and give a balanced view of the proposals for and against change. This point was also litigated in *Jordan v Referendum Act 1994*,[22] regarding the information booklet presented by the Minister for Children in advance of the Children's Referendum. However, the case was subsequently rejected. Barrington J's decision in *Hanafin v Minister for the Environment*[23] clearly sets out the jurisprudence of the court on the issue of setting aside referendum results.

---

[19] [1976] IR 38.
[20] [1995] 2 IR 10.
[21] Also, see the discussion on referendum petitions in the referendum process at section 8.1.3
[22] [2015] IESC 33
[23] [1996] 2 IR 321.

> "The court will not lightly set aside what appears, prima facie, to be an Act of the sovereign people. Unless, therefore, what has happened is an expression and obvious Constitutional abuse affecting the outcome of the Referendum, the onus of proof on the petitioner will be a heavy one."[24]

Adding that:

> "The Government was guilty of a Constitutional wrong, but this wrong was discovered before the date of the referendum and the people voted with full knowledge of what the Government had done."[25]

Therefore, equality for the purposes of balancing speech in cases of referendums through State expenditure, is something that must be pursued by the government, and they cannot support one side over the other. However, this will not be enough for a referendum result to be overturned, as it is not significant enough for it to amount to a material defect in the referendum process.[26]

## 7.5 Right to Life

The right to life in the Irish Constitution is expressly stated in Art 40.3.2°. It may surprise some to realise that even this right is not absolute. In the time of creating the Constitution, the death penalty was still exercised in Ireland. At the time, suicide was a criminal offence. Also, the right to self-defence for the protection of life contemplates the taking of the life of another to protect another life. Under common law, a person is permitted to use force, including lethal force to protect his life or the life of another. So, therefore, there are clear restrictions on the right to life.[27] However, these are not the most contentious elements of the right to life: these issues are abortion and euthanasia. The current friction in the law relates to the autonomy of individuals, their right to self-determination, and their ability to either end their own life with the assistance of another in the case of euthanasia, or the determination of the point of life beginning regarding the unborn child. The right to life could be considered to reflect the natural law perspective of the constitution.

---

[24] *Hanafin v Minister for the Environment* [1996] 2 IR 321 at 456- 457.
[25] *ibid* at 457- 458.
[26] See amendment of the constitution for a further discussion on the process of referendums at section 8.1.
[27] *People (Attorney General) v Dwyer* [1972] IR 416.

### 7.5.1 The Death Penalty

The death penalty was a traditional punishment for those who took the life of another. In Ireland, the imposition of the death penalty was gradually constrained to the offence of capital murder. Capital murder is the unlawful killing of a member of the Gardaí or Defence Forces in the exercise of their duty. The majority of the sentences were commuted to life imprisonment. In 1990, the Criminal Justice Act 1990 abolished the use of the death penalty, yet it still remained as part of the Constitution. In 2001, due to international commitments, the Constitution was amended to create an express prohibition on the use of the death penalty. Now, under Art 15.5.2° the Oireachtas is prevented from using the death penalty for any offence even in times of war or emergency. Even if emergency powers are exercised in the State, the death penalty cannot be used under the terms of Art 28.3.

The importance of prohibiting the death penalty even in times of emergencies is important. During such "emergency" times the provisions of the Constitution are suspended in order to protect national security or the integrity of the State. Such emergency situations arose during the Second World War and the escalation of the Northern Ireland situation in the 1970s. In both instances, there was an external and an internal threat of invasion or the overthrow of democratic order in the State. The decree of an emergency allows for the personal rights of the citizen to be put on hold in order to protect democracy in the State. For example, the right to freedom of expression may be completely curtailed in case people may be using this right to seek for the overthrow of the State.

### 7.5.2 The Right to Life and the Unborn Child

Abortion is one of the most contentious issues in contemporary Ireland. Prior to 1983, Ireland had the exact same provisions dealing with abortion as the United Kingdom. The only prohibition on abortion was contained in the Offences against the Person Act 1861 which made the provision or procurement of an abortion a criminal offence. There was no constitutional section dealing with abortion. However, the US judgment of *Roe v Wade*[28] judicially interpreted the right to an abortion into the US Constitution as a privacy right. Considering the development of privacy rights in Ireland through *McGee*,[29] anti-abortion campaigners lobbied the government for the insertion of a right to life of the unborn into the Constitution to prevent a similar judgment in Ireland. The political background to the time had been

---

[28]  410 US 113 (1973).
[29]  [1974] IR 284; see also the right to privacy at section 7.3.3.1.

revolving governments between the major parties on a six monthly basis.

The current Constitutional protection for the unborn child is stated in Art 40.3.3°:

> "The State acknowledges the right to life of the unborn and, with due regard to the equal right to life of the mother, guarantees in its law to respect, and, as far as practicable, by its laws to defend and vindicate that right.
>
> This subsection shall not limit freedom to travel between the State and another State.
>
> This subsection shall not limit freedom to obtain or make available in the State, subject to such conditions as may be laid down by law, information relating to services lawfully available in another state."

Many side issues have been litigated through the right to life of the unborn child, such as the right to information[30] and the right to travel which formed part of one set of referendum proposals to the people regarding abortion following the $X$[31] case judgment in December 1992. This is the reason for the qualification sections of the article which reduce the ability of the court to read in extra protections to protect the life of the unborn child by the mother travelling to other jurisdictions for the procurement of an abortion.

The first problem that is faced when dealing with abortion is the point at which life begins. The closest definition which the court has given on this point was in *Attorney General (Society for the Protection of the Unborn Child (Ireland) Ltd) v Open Door Counselling Ltd*,[32] where Hamilton P looked at s 58 and 59 of the Offences Against the Person Act 1861 which operated against a woman who had conceived a child. Therefore the point of conception was determined as the point at which the "unborn child" is protected by law. This definition also has implications for scientific research in Ireland specifically in relation to embryo research and stem cells. However, in *MR v TR*,[33] it was held that embryos created and stored outside of the womb did not attract the protection of the 8th Amendment of the Constitution.

---

[30] See section 7.5.2 on the judicial interpretation of the right to abortion information considering the position of the unborn child in the Irish Constitution.

[31] [1992] 1 IR 1.

[32] [1988] IR 593.

[33] [2006] IEHC 359.

The judgment of X was the most prolific judgment relating to abortion in Ireland. In the case, X was a 14-year-old girl who had been raped by her neighbour. She became pregnant and threatened to commit suicide. As a result, the girl and her family travelled to England to procure an abortion. As the neighbour was denying responsibility, the family contacted Gardaí to ask if they needed any material from the abortion to aid in the prosecution of the neighbour. As the Gardaí were informed, the Attorney General then sought an injunction to restrain X from travelling to England. The family was already in Fishguard and agreed to travel home. The subsequent case was to make Ireland subject of international criticism and challenge traditional assumptions surrounding abortion in Ireland. The High Court agreed with the injunction. However, the Supreme Court was to make a historic judgment.

In the Supreme Court, Finlay CJ held that if there is a real and substantial risk to the life, as distinct to the health, of the mother, then a termination of pregnancy is permissible according to Art 40.3.3°. In the X case, suicide was held to be permissible ground for an abortion. McCarthy, O'Flaherty and Egan JJ also agreed with this formulation. The sole dissenting judgment came from Hederman J. The essence of the judgment is that the life of the child is contingent on the continuing health and life of the mother who is a life in being. Therefore, it could be argued that this judgment did not see eye to eye with the equal life of the mother and unborn child as rhetoric but a practical balancing between the life of the mother who is required to give sustenance to a life contingent on the continued survival of the mother. This position was reaffirmed in *A and B v Eastern Health Board*,[34] where the parents of rape victims in State care tried to prevent their children from procuring abortions with the assistance of the State. In these cases, the State agencies were allowed to procure abortions for those in their care where the individuals concerned fell within the X criteria.

The issue of fatal foetal abnormality arose in *D v Health Service Executive*.[35] In this case, a pregnant child in the care of the State learned that her unborn child would not survive outside of the womb due to a condition known as anencephaly. The High Court ruled that the HSE could not prevent the girl from travelling to the United Kingdom, but the abortion could not be carried out in Ireland. This situation where the foetus' condition is not compatible with life has received much media attention in recent times. However, the Protection of Life During Pregnancy Act 2013 does not make any provision for such intervention to be made in Ireland. A referendum is to be held on 25 May 2018 to

---

[34] [1988] 1 IR 464.
[35] Unreported, High Court, McKechnie J, 9 May 2007.

repeal the provisions of the 8th Amendment following the report of the Citizens' Assembly[36] and the report of the Joint Oireachtas Committee Report on 8th Amendment of the Constitution.[37]

The 36th Amendment of the Constitution Bill 2018 which has been approved by the Oireachtas provides for Art 40.3.3° to be replaced with the following text: "Provision may be made by law for the regulation of termination of pregnancy".[38]

The Department of Health[39] has published a policy document for the legislation which would regulate the provision of terminations if the referendum is successful. The envisaged legislation which would emanate from this policy document would provide for terminations on health grounds, where there is a risk to health in an emergency situation, fatal foetal conditions, and terminations up to 12 weeks. The policy document also provides for conscientious objections by medical practitioners, repeal of the Protection in Life During Pregnancy Act 2013 and the creation of reporting structures on terminations if the 8th Amendment is repealed.

As regards the State's ability to protect the unborn child in delivery, a number of interesting judgments have been handed down. In *HSE v B*,[40] a mother wished to opt for a natural delivery of her child with a willingness to consent to a caesarean delivery where natural delivery was not possible. However, the HSE sought an injunction to force the woman to deliver her child by caesarean as her previous children had been born this way. Even on the basis of the medical evidence presented, and the risk to the life of the unborn child, Twomey J held that the increased risk by natural birth was not enough to "justify this Court in effectively authorising her to have her uterus opened against her will, something which would constitute a grievous assault if it were done on a woman who was not pregnant",[41] adding "that it is a step too far to order the forced caesarean section of a woman against her

---

36  https://www.citizensassembly.ie/en/The-Eighth-Amendment-of-the-Constitution/Final-Report-on-the-Eighth-Amendment-of-the-Constitution/Final-Report-incl-Appendix-A-D.pdf accessed 12 March 2018.

37  https://data.oireachtas.ie/ie/oireachtas/committee/dail/32/joint_committee_on_the_eighth_amendment_of_the_constitution/reports/2017/2017-12-20_report-of-the-joint-committee-on-the-eighth-amendment-of-the-constitution_en.pdf accessed 12 March 2018.

38  http://www.oireachtas.ie/documents/bills28/bills/2018/2918/b2918d.pdf accessed 12 March 2018.

39  http://health.gov.ie/wp-content/uploads/2018/03/Policy-paper-approved-by-Goverment-8-March-2018.pdf accessed 12 March 2018.

40  [2016] IEHC 605.

41  *ibid* at para 19.

will, even though not making that order increases the risk of injury and death to both Ms. B and her unborn child."[42]

In *A, B and C v Ireland*,[43] Ireland was found to be in breach of the European Convention on Human Rights in respect of its abortion regime. As part of the agreed Programme for Government, both Fine Gael and Labour agreed to convene an expert group to assess the implications from the judgment.[44] The recommendations from this report were to be contained in Protection of Life During Pregnancy Act 2013. This legislation has been criticised for not addressing the core problem, which was the construction of the 8th Amendment, being unworkable in cases of mental health issues, and not dealing with the issues of fatal foetal abnormalities.

In *PP v HSE*,[45] the court had to rule on whether a life support machine for an expectant brain-dead young woman could be turned off even though this would result in the death of the foetus. The plaintiff was the father of the woman (NP) and sought the courts leave to allow for his daughter to die a natural death, but this was complicated by the constitutional position of the unborn child. The HSE intended to keep NP on life support for the duration of the pregnancy to "facilitate the continuation of maternal organ supportive measures in an attempt to attain foetal viability".[46] Her pregnancy was at 15 weeks at that stage. The court held that in the circumstances of the case, notwithstanding the constitutional protection for the unborn child:

> "[t]o maintain and continue the present somatic support for the mother would deprive her of dignity in death and subject her father, her partner and her young children to unimaginable distress in a futile exercise which commenced only because of fears held by treating medical specialists of potential legal consequences. Highly experienced medical practitioners with the best interests of both mother and unborn child in mind do not believe there is any medical or ethically based reason for continuing with a process which

---

[42] [2016] IEHC 605 at para 21.

[43] *A, B and C v Ireland* App No 25579/05 (ECtHR, 16 December 2010), available at http://hudoc.echr.coe.int/sites/eng/pages/search.aspx?i=001-102332 (accessed 21 February 2014).

[44] The expert group is mentioned under the heading "Bioethics" in Department of the Taoiseach, *Programme for Government 2011–2016* (2011), available at http://www.taoiseach.gov.ie/eng/Work_Of_The_Department/Programme_for_Government/Programme_for_Government_2011-2016.pdf (accessed 21 April 2014).

[45] [2014] IEHC 622.

[46] *ibid.*

Dr McKenna described as verging on the grotesque on the particular facts in this case."[47]

### 7.5.3 Abortion Information

The right to information was construed in the case of *The Attorney General (The Society for the Protection of Unborn Children Ireland Ltd) v Open Door Counselling Ltd and Dublin Wellwoman Centre Ltd.*[48] The primary issue in the case was the provisions of information regarding abortion services, which services were available in England but were repugnant to the Irish Constitution under Art 40.3.3° as constituted at the time of the action.[49] This action was taken before the $X$[50] case and the constitutional amendments that took place after that case. The judgment of Finlay CJ touched on the idea of an implied right to the dissemination of information contained in the wording of Art 40.6.1°; commenting on Law Reform Commission Report, Finlay CJ cited the following excerpt:

> "It was further suggested that the right to receive and give information which, it was alleged, existed and was material to this case was, though not expressly granted, impliedly referred to or involved in the right of citizens to express freely their convictions and opinions provided by Article 40, s. 6, sub-s. 1 of the Constitution, since, it was claimed, the right to express freely convictions and opinions may, under some circumstances, involve as an ancillary right the right to obtain information. I am satisfied that no right could constitutionally arise to obtain information the purpose of the obtaining of which was to defeat the constitutional right to life of the unborn child."[51]

This ground of appeal was defeated as the nature of the information being sought for the procurement of an abortion in the State was to go against the right to life of the unborn child. The judgment of Denham J in *Society for the Protection of the Unborn Child v Grogan (No.5)*[52] considered the general right to information. From *A.G. (S.P.U.C.) v Open Door Counselling Ltd,*[53] it had been established that there was no right to information for a purpose contrary to the Constitution:

---

[47]   *ibid.*
[48]   *Attorney General (The Society for the Protection of Unborn Children Ireland Ltd) v Open Door Counselling Ltd and Dublin Wellwoman Centre Ltd* [1988] 1 IR 593.
[49]   See now the Protection of Life During Pregnancy Act 2013.
[50]   *The Attorney General v X* [1992] 1 IR 1.
[51]   *A.G. (S.P.U.C.) v Open Door Counselling Ltd* [1988] 1 IR 593 at 625.
[52]   [1998] 4 IR 343.
[53]   [1988] IR 593.

"It is illogical and incorrect to analyse the situation and determine that there can be no information given to or received by a party to actions that may include situations where the actions are lawful. ... To deny a right under the Constitution to information on the basis that another constitutional right exists, without any attempt at harmonising the rights, is to fall into error."[54]

In the case law discussed above, the right of the unborn child, as framed in Art 40.3.3°, is in competition with the right to life of the mother. The broader argument, which is investigated in this thesis, concerns the competing claims of the citizens and the government in relation to policy information. The power held by the government to govern is through the citizen, yet to protect this form of rule there may be legitimate matters which need to be shielded from the citizen. Therefore, the balance which must be achieved between the sentiments of the constitutional framing of government and the reality of power is a delicate one. This can only be achieved with a harmonious interpretation of the roles and powers of both the government and citizens.

### 7.5.4 Right to Die

The closest that the Irish legal system has come to recognising the right to die is in the case law on the right to die a natural death. The legislature decriminalised suicide in the Criminal Law (Suicide) Act 1993. However, a person aiding another in committing suicide would still be subject to prosecution either as manslaughter or murder, and if found to be assisting under the Act, would be potentially subject to 14 years' imprisonment. Therefore, there is no constitutional right to die by artificial means or through medical intervention.

The courts have found that there is an unenumerated right to die a natural death in the Constitution. In the case of *In Re a Ward of Court (withholding medical treatment) (No. 2),*[55] the Supreme Court held that the family of a women in a near persistent vegetative state was permitted to ask for the feeding tube that was her sole means of nutrition be removed after 23 years to allow her to die a natural death. The ward had no control over her bodily movements and she had suffered severe brain damage. Her family wanted her to be able to die with dignity. In the case of such an individual, or someone without the mental capacity to make decisions for themselves is at issue, the court will make the person a ward of court. This means that the family will not

---

[54]  [1998] 4 IR 3 at 374.
[55]  [1996] 2 IR 79.

be the final arbiters of their relatives' lives, and instead the court will step in to act in the best interests of the individual concerned. In this case, a distinction can be made between assisted suicide and allowing an individual to pass with dignity. Traditionally, the courts have been willing to allow for death to happen naturally by removing means of supporting life without actively bringing about death. As stated by Hamilton CJ in *In Re a Ward (withholding medical treatment) (No. 2)*[56]:

> "As the process of dying is part, and an ultimate inevitable consequence, of life, the right to life necessarily implies the right to have nature take its course and to die a natural death and, unless the individual concerned so wishes, not to have life artificially maintained by the provision of nourishment by abnormal artificial means, which have no curative effect and which is intended merely to prolong life.
>
> This right, as so defined, does not include the right to have life terminated or death accelerated and is confined to the natural process of dying. No person has the right to terminate or to have terminated his or her life or to accelerate or have accelerated his or her life."

In *Fleming v Ireland, AG and DPP*,[57] the applicant was a multiple sclerosis suffer who sought to challenge, in the High Court, the constitutionality and compatibility of s 2(2) of the Criminal Law (Suicide) Act 1993 with regard to assisted suicide and if her challenge was unsuccessful, that the DPP would draw up guidelines as to prosecution of those that assist with someone taking their own life. The appeal to the Supreme Court solely concerned the constitutionality of the legislation and its compatibility with the Convention on Human Rights. Denham J distinguished the case at hand to the *In Re a Ward of Court (withholding medical treatment) (No.2)*[58] case, as it centred on the withholding of treatment, as opposed to a positive act to end the life of another. The absence of a right to die in the Constitution was stated clearly "There is no explicit right to commit suicide, or to determine the time of one's death, in the Constitution."[59]

Outside of the argument related to the right to life, the applicant argued that the legislative prohibition infringed on her right

> "to personal and bodily autonomy and self-determination:

---

[56]  *In Re a Ward (withholding medical treatment) (No. 2)* [1996] 2 IR 79 at 124.
[57]  [2013] IESC 19.
[58]  [1996] 2 IR 79.
[59]  [2013] IESC 19, para 99.

specifically her right to make and carry out decisions about her own life including death; her right to privacy, her right to live (including her right to die) (and) her right to be held equal with other citizens before the law".[60]

The court stated that constitutional rights exist "of general application for the benefit of every citizen and person entitled to assert such rights" but it is not "the jurisprudence of the Irish Constitution that rights can be identified for a limited group of persons in particular circumstances no matter how tragic and heartrending they may be".[61]

However, Denham CJ did state that it would be possible for the Oireachtas to legislate for such issues as those in the *Fleming* case in the future if it wished to do so:

"Nothing in this judgment should be taken as necessarily implying that it would not be open to the State, in the event that the Oireachtas were satisfied that measures with appropriate safeguards could be introduced, to legislate to deal with a case such as that of the appellant. If such legislation was introduced it would be for the courts to determine whether the balancing by the Oireachtas of any legitimate concerns was within the boundaries of what was constitutionally permissible. Any such consideration would, necessarily, have to pay appropriate regard to the assessment made by the Oireachtas both of any competing interests and the practicability of any measures thus introduced."[62]

## 7.6 Civil and Political Rights

The right to freedom of expression for political speech is to be found as an enumerated right in the text of Art 40.6.1° where the full protection for freedom of expression is split over two articles. Article 40.6.1° covers freedom of expression in connection to the discussion of government policy and Art 40.3.1° has been used to develop a liberal unenumerated speech right. The citizen's freedom to debate matters of government policy is extremely important to the functioning of a democracy, as it is interlinked with the concept of representative democracy[63] under which the democratic order of the Irish State seeks

---

[60] *ibid*, para 109.
[61] *ibid*, para 115.
[62] *ibid*, para 108.
[63] This form of democracy is envisaged by Art 16.2.1° of the Constitution,

to find its validity by virtue of Art 6.1.[64] This could be argued as a reason why Art 40.6.1° specifically mentions its role in this regard.[65]

The personal rights of the citizen under the Irish Constitution are to be found in the broad provisions of Art 40. These rights are also referred to as the fundamental rights of the citizen. Article 40.6.1° makes specific reference to the liberty for the exercise of a number of rights. These rights are expressions of convictions and opinions,[66] the right to assemble peacefully and without arms,[67] and the formation of association and unions.[68] These rights are generally collectively referred to as the civil and political rights. They directly affect political protest, speech and the formation of parties and unions which have an influence on the direction of governance and political protest in a democracy. Article 40.6.1° (i) incorporates the "criticism of government policy" as part of the rightful liberty of expression that is bestowed on the organs of public opinion in their mandate of educating public opinion. This is in line with the general tenor of the rights incorporated in the general framework of Art 40.6.1°. This is not the sole source for a right to freedom of expression within the constitutional framework. The interpretation of the unenumerated rights pursuant to Art 40.3.1° has also led the creation of a liberal right to communication in *Attorney General v Paperlink*.[69] Therefore, the Irish right to freedom of expression has both a liberal and a political expression in the constitution and both need to be examined in turn.

### 7.6.1 The Political Right to Freedom of Expression

The right to freedom of expression has been given a particular political construction from the interpretation of Art 40.6.1°. This is due to a specific reference to the right "to express freely convictions and opinions"[70] but also the role of the media in the exercise of political expression. The media's role as a conduit of public discourse

---

which states that "Dáil Éireann shall be composed of members who represent constituencies determined by law."

[64] "All powers of government, legislative, executive and judicial, derive, under God, from the people, whose right it is to designate the rulers of the State and, in final appeal, to decide all questions of national policy, according to the requirements of the common good."

[65] The Constitution Committee of 1934 was focused on the assembly aspect of the old Art 9 and the ability of the police to deal with meetings that were designed to cause a breach of the peace. G Hogan, *The Origins of the Irish Constitution* (Royal Irish Academy, Dublin, 2012), p 39.

[66] Art 40.6.1°(i).

[67] Art 40.6.1°(ii).

[68] Art 40.6.1°(iii).

[69] *Attorney General v Paperlink* [1984] ILRM 373.

[70] Art 40.6.1°(i).

is acknowledged. The Constitution imbues them with a particular role as the "educators of public opinion". The exercise of this role is specifically protected with the regard to the "criticism of government policy". The only restriction placed on the right in the Article is in connection with the protection of public order and morality. However, the media clause is subject to the restriction of the "authority of the state". Furthermore, the whole clause is finished off with the three speech crimes of blasphemy, sedition and obscenity, which are also restrictions, but not central to the discussion of political speech freedoms.

The wording of this Article does contain a number of complexities.[71] The phrasing of the restrictions in connection with government policy may not create a positive right, and there is no obligation on the government to facilitate or encourage the criticism of government policy. The wording of the Article only restrains the legislature from placing impediments in the way of citizens criticising government policy, especially via the media. The second paragraph of the Article relates in its entirety to the organs of public opinion, in other words, the media. At the time of drafting of the Article, the media was solely comprised of the radio, cinema and the press. The media has since evolved and now includes television and the internet. Regarding "organs of public opinion" and whether there is a divergence in protection between the citizen and the media, Barrington J held that:

> "it would be absurd to suggest that the press enjoys constitutional protection under Article 40.6.1(i) when criticising government policy but not when reporting the facts on which its criticism is based".[72]

Furthermore, Barrington J stated that it would seem "absurd to suggest that the constitutional right of the citizens to express freely their convictions and opinions does not also protect, subject to constitutional exceptions, their right to state facts".[73]

At the time of drafting the 1937 Constitution, there were concerns

---

[71] These complexities are also referred to by O Doyle. Doyle also questions the construction of the right of the free speech guarantee in the Constitution regarding the express statement of certain aspects to the citizen and the statement of the remainder of the rights regarding the media. O Doyle, *Constitutional Law: Text, Cases and Materials* (Clarus Press, Dublin, 2008), p 198. This point is also referenced by Patrick Dillon-Malone in "Privacy and Media Law" in U Kilkelly (ed.) *ECHR and Irish Law* (Jordans, Bristol, 2004).

[72] *Irish Times v Ireland* [1998] 1 IR 359 at 406; see also the discussion regarding *Murphy v Independent Radio and Television Commission* [1999] 1 IR 12 later in this section.

[73] *Irish Times v Ireland* [1998] 1 IR 359 at 406.

voiced by the Institute of Journalists that the provision to restrict speech in order to ensure that the media was not used as a means to undermine the authority of the State was "dangerously wide, and ambiguous, and could be used as a cover to interfere with the rights of journalists and constitute a menace to the liberty of the press".[74]

The emphasis in the Article is actually on the undermining of public order, morality or the authority of the State. Therefore, the primary objective of the Article was to prevent the organs of public opinion from being used to overthrow this order. It could be argued that the mention of freedom of expression, and in turn the criticism of government policy, is really a secondary aim of the paragraph to balance the restriction in question. Therefore, it could be argued that due to these concerns, the clear statement of the right to political speech may have been viewed as secondary to the primary concerns of the drafters.

The Constitutional Law Review Group felt that the framing of Art 40.6.1° (i) was in order to protect the substance of the right but to allow it to be qualified in certain circumstances. Nevertheless, the wording was described by McGonagle[75] as "qualified and ambivalent". Also, Hogan and Whyte contend that the Group

> "in particular...considered that the right to free expression should not be subject to the test of 'public order or morality or the authority of the State' as this test was too all-embracing."[76]

In *Irish Times v Ireland*,[77] the judgment of Barrington J touched on the level of facilitation required for freedom of expression. It was held that the right to freedom of expression was a "positive right which the State is pledged to defend".[78] He further stated that a "function of the court is to preserve the balance ... in such a way as to give to the right guaranteed life and reality". Barrington J also emphasised the differences between the Irish protection and that of a common law

---

[74] Letter from JW Kelly to Eamon de Valera representing the Committee of the Dublin and Irish Association District of the Institute of Journalists (No 212: NAI, DT S9931A), as reproduced in G Hogan, *The Origins of the Irish Constitution* (Royal Irish Academy, Dublin, 2012), p 588.

[75] "Freedom of Expression and Information", in G Quinn, *Irish Human Rights Yearbook* (Round Hall Press, Dublin, 1995), p 130.

[76] G Hogan and G Whyte, *JM Kelly: The Irish Constitution* (4th ed, Tottel Publishing, Dublin, 2006), p 1779.

[77] [1998] 1 IR 359.

[78] *ibid.*

country where "the citizen is entitled to say anything he wishes as long as it is not illegal".[79]

This judgment highlighted the debate surrounding the constitutional framing of the right as a negative right[80] or as a positive right that the State must protect. The best interpretation of the article in the Irish context may be that the right is actually a neutral right; it must be vindicated where necessary, yet the State may not do anything to fetter the exercise of the right.[81] Therefore, it could be adduced that the right should be facilitated in so far as practicable in a proportionate manner. In the course of the judgment, Barrington J further stated that the context of the right, amongst the fundamental rights, is important to its interpretation. He stated that the rights that are related to freedom of expression in the constitutional landscape all related to the "public activities of the citizen and ... the practical workings of a democratic society (forming) part of the dynamics of political change"[82]. Barrington J then got to the core of the issue in the following statement, "they are at once both vitally important to the success of a democracy and potentially a source of political instability."[83]

In the case of *Murphy v Independent Radio and Television Commission*,[84] the applicant sought judicial review of the decision of the respondent commission to restrict the broadcast of a radio advertisement by the applicant. In Barrington J's judgment, reference was made to the grouping of freedom of expression, freedom of assembly and the right to join associations together in Art 40.6.1. In the High Court, Geoghegan J expressed his "puzzlement" at such an arrangement.[85] In the Supreme Court, Barrington J stated that:

---

[79] *ibid.*

[80] See also L Alexander, *Is there a Right to Freedom of Expression?* (Cambridge University Press, Cambridge, 2005), p 4.

[81] The judgment of Budd J in *Educational Company of Ireland Ltd v Fitzpatrick (No. 2)* [1961] IR 345 at 368 would also back up this assertion: "If an established right in law exists a citizen has the right to assert it and it is the duty of the Courts to aid and assist him in the assertion of his right. The Court will therefore assist and uphold a citizen's constitutional rights. Obedience to the law is required of every citizen, and it follows that if one citizen has a right under the Constitution there exists a correlative duty on the part of other citizens to respect that right and not to interfere with it. To say otherwise would be tantamount to saying that a citizen can set the Constitution at naught and that a right solemnly given by our fundamental law is valueless. It follows that the Courts will not so act as to permit anybody of citizens to deprive another of his constitutional rights and will in any proceedings before them see that these rights are protected, whether they be assailed under the guise of a statutory right or otherwise."

[82] [1998] 1 IR 359 at 404.

[83] *ibid* at 404.

[84] *Murphy v Independent Radio and Television Commission* [1999] 1 IR 12.

[85] *ibid* at 17.

"the framers of the Constitution had deliberately included them in the one sub-section for a reason. Geoghegan J drew the conclusion that the reason was that they were concerned with the influencing of public opinions."[86]

Furthermore, Geoghegan J in the High Court, contended that the provisions of Art 40.6.1° "did not seem to have any application to the right of a private citizen to express private opinions with a view to influencing some other person or persons."[87] Barrington J, in the Supreme Court, was of the opinion that the rights were grouped in such a fashion as they concerned the "public activities of the citizen in a democratic society".[88]

The Law Reform Commission Report on the Civil Law of Defamation in 1991 specifically addressed the complexities in the interpretation of Art 40.6.1°. In relation to the Dáil Debates on the Constitution, the Commission drew attention to the second part of the Article in relation to the limitation pertaining to public order and morality.[89] The Commission stated that "it was felt by some deputies that this (provision) had potential for becoming a means of curtailing government criticism".[90] With regard to the education of public opinion, it was suggested that the phrase "was misconceived, it being thought that opinion should be allowed to compete with each other and that this was preferable to a set of opinions being approved in some sense by the State".[91]

The most recent case to discuss the direct link between freedom of expression and political debate was that of *Doherty v Referendum Commission*.[92] In this case, the judgment of Hogan J considered the link between the role of the citizen under Art 6.1 and the construction of Art 40.6.1°. Hogan J stated that the nature of Art 6.1 created the form of popular sovereignty where citizens were to be called on to make "critical decisions",[93] that Art 40.6.1° envisaged "informed citizenry",[94] and where referendums encouraged the citizens to "engage in robust political debate so that the forces of deliberation will prevail over the arbitrary and irrational so that, in this civic democracy, reasoned

---

[86] *ibid* at 17.
[87] *ibid* at 17.
[88] [1999] 1 IR 12 at 24.
[89] Also see E O'Dell, "Reflections on a Revolution in Libel" (2012) 30 ILT 1.
[90] Law Reform Commission, *The Report on the Civil Law of Defamation* (LRC 38–1991), p 114.
[91] *ibid* at p 114.
[92] [2012] IEHC 211.
[93] *ibid* at para 21.
[94] *ibid* at para 24.

argument would prevail in this triumph of discourse".[95] It was also stated that under the provisions of Art 9.3 that the Constitution placed a "premium on honest and fearless debate" in times of referenda.[96]

Even though Ireland already had a written statement of the right to political speech, the judgments of Fennelly J in both *Mahon v Keena*[97] and *Mahon v Post Publications*[98] relied significantly upon the provisions of Art 10 of the European Convention of Human Rights and barely mention the applicable norms of common law or, indeed, the Constitution. It must be accepted that these cases were predominantly centred on the concept of journalistic privilege, which was an alien concept to the provisions of the Constitution. However, the willingness to place such heavy reliance on Art 10 shows how the gaps in the original constitutional construction for political speech can be enhanced by the Convention. Fennelly J in both *Mahon* cases implies that Art 40.6.1°(i) is receptive soil for Art 10 analysis.[99]

In *Mahon v Post Publications*, Fennelly J in considering the right to freedom of expression took a cursory note of the *Paperlink*[100] and *Murphy*[101] in order to elucidate the constitutional provisions, but then moved straight to an analysis of Art 10. Fennelly J clearly stated that the "area must now be considered in light of the European Convention on Human Rights Act 2003".[102] The learned judge also found the Irish proportionality approach to be "closely comparable to that adopted by the European Court of Human Rights when interpreting the Convention".[103]

A comparative approach based on the provisions of Art 10 of the European Convention on Human Rights, amongst other comparative jurisprudence, was also attempted in *Hunter v Duckworth*[104] on the grounds of qualified privilege. However, *Mahon v Keena*[105] was to ground its judgment on Art 10 to the extent that the application of the Convention comprised of seven pages of the judgment. The

---

[95]   *ibid* at para 23.
[96]   *ibid* at para 22.
[97]   *Mahon v Keena* [2010] 1 IR 336.
[98]   *Mahon v Post Publications* [2007] IESC 15.
[99]   Indeed, there are pre-incorporation cases which made the same point, if more weakly; see *State (DPP) v Walsh* [1981] IR 412 at 440 (Henchy J); *Desmond v Glackin (No 1)* [1992] 2 ILRM 490 (O'Hanlon J); *Wong v Minister for Justice* [1994] 1 IR 223 (Denham J).
[100]  *Attorney General v Paperlink* [1984] ILRM 373.
[101]  *Murphy v Independent Television and Radio Commission* [1999] 1 IR 12.
[102]  *Mahon v Post Publications* [2007] IESC 15, para 46.
[103]  *ibid* at para 54.
[104]  *Hunter v Gerald Duckworth & Co Ltd.* [2003] IEHC 81.
[105]  *Mahon v Keena* [2010] 1 IR 336.

learned judge also sought to compare the relevant law of the United States to the case at hand. In a heavy reliance on the provisions of Art 10 and on similar facts to *Mahon v Post Publications*, Fennelly J reiterated the importance of the press and the grounding of a right to journalistic privilege as part of the protections for political speech in the Convention and therefore, expanded the provision of this privilege to the Irish jurisdiction.

### 7.6.2 A Right to Information?

Commentators now consider that it is clear from judgments concerning Art 40.6.1°(i) that the provisions of the article also include a right to the dissemination of information as intrinsic to the right to express opinions.[106] This is based on the judgments of both Costello J[107] and Keane J[108] in some of the landmark cases which interpreted the provisions of Art 40.6.1°.

In *O'Brien v Mirror Group Newspapers Ltd*,[109] Denham J did imply the right to information into the wording of the constitutional guarantee when making a comparison between the right to freedom of expression envisaged in the terms of Art 40.6.1°(i) and a comparative analysis to the freedoms incorporated into Art 10 of the European Convention on Humans Rights. Denham J stated that both require a balance and issues such as "information, communications and the freedom of expression are a matter of importance in a democracy and is of public interest".[110] *Cornec v Morrice*[111] has revisited the issue of information

---

[106] G Hogan and G Whyte, *JM Kelly: The Irish Constitution* (4th ed, Tottel Publishing, Dublin, 2006), p 1726.

[107] Specifically Costello J in *Attorney General v Paperlink* [1984] ILRM 373, and *Kearney v Minister for Justice* [1986] IR 116, [1987] ILRM 52, even though the *Paperlink* case, refers to the right to communicate without reference to a political speech argument. For example, whether A can communicate with B by giving B information (letters, a broadcast, etc), not with whether A can communicate by getting information from B. However, it is arguable that a right to information might be derived from Art 40.3 by analogy with these cases, or as a necessary corollary of the right in these cases. Taking these cases in line with the argument surrounding a tenuous right to official information, it may be possible to constitutionally ground an argument to recognise a right to political information, especially when the argument surrounding the interpretation of Art 6.1 is incorporated.

[108] Specifically Keane J in *Oblique Financial Services v The Promise Productions Co Ltd* [1994] 1 ILRM 74, *O'Laoire v The Medical Council*, unreported, High Court, Keane J, 27 January 1995, *Carrigaline Community Television Broadcasting Co Ltd v The Minister for Transport Energy and Communications (No. 2)* [1997] 1 ILRM 241 and *Society for the Protection of the Unborn Child (Ireland) Ltd v Grogan (No.5)* [1998] 4 IR 343.

[109] *O'Brien v Mirror Group Newspapers Ltd* [2001] 1 IR 1.

[110] *ibid.*

[111] *ibid.*

and public debate. The case surrounded a company law issue in the jurisdiction of Colorado but the plaintiffs wished to examine the sources of Irish journalism on the issue. In the judgment of Hogan J, the right to information was important to exercise the constitutional rights envisaged in Art 40.6.1°(i). The learned judge stated that

> "these constitutional fundamentals have been overlooked at times, in part possibly because the syntax and drafting of this particular clause is (uncharacteristically) awkward given that the critical proviso is somewhat obscured by being placed within a subordinate clause".[112]

Therefore, there is a gathering momentum that the right to freedom of expression contains an implied right to information which has developed from *Cullen* to *Cornec* today.

It could be argued that this jurisprudential evolution has more to do with the implications of the European Convention on Human Rights protections into the spirit of the Constitution in order to provide for a basic commonality in freedom of expression protection as opposed to a broadening of protection in the Constitution in its own right.

### 7.6.3 Blasphemy and Freedom of Expression

Morality is listed as one of the permissible restrictions on the right to freedom of expression. Morality can be considered as blasphemy and is itself subject to its own provision in the framing of the free speech article.

Article 40.6.1° is the main constitutional provision for freedom of expression and states that citizens are granted the right to freely express their convictions and opinions. However, the exercise of this right is restricted if the expression in question is blasphemous and can be punished in law. The Article in itself does not define what is blasphemous. The Defamation Act of 2009 sets out the definition of what is considered to be blasphemous under the provisions of s 36(2) which states that:

> "(a) he or she publishes or utters matter that is grossly abusive or insulting in relation to matters held sacred by any religion, thereby causing outrage among a substantial number of the adherents of that religion, and

---

[112] *ibid* at para 42.

(b) he or she intends, by the publication or utterance of the matter concerned, to cause such outrage."

The defences contained in s 36(3) allows for a defendant to prove that a reasonable person would find genuine literary, artistic, political, scientific, or academic value in the matter to which the offence relates.

In *Corway v Independent Newspapers*,[113] the applicant sought leave to commence criminal proceedings against the Independent Group and the *Sunday Independent's* Editor for blasphemous libel. In the affidavit, the applicant stated that because of the publication of the cartoon in the Sunday Independent he suffered "offence and outrage by reason of the insult, ridicule and contempt shown towards the sacrament of the Eucharist".[114] The offending element of the Sunday publication was a cartoon by Wendy Shea with the title "Hello Progress–Bye Bye Father" with an article questioning the influence of the Catholic Church in Ireland after the successful campaign to allow for divorce. The tag line used for the caption was a play on the posters that were used in opposition to the Referendum to allow for divorce. These posters had the tag line of "Hello Divorce–Bye Bye Daddy". The cartoon caricatured three government ministers rejecting the Host and Chalice being offered by a priest.

This application was refused by Geoghegan J in the High Court as there was no prima facie case to be answered in the opinion of Geoghegan J. He further stated that even if there was a case to answered, leave would not have been granted as it was felt that there would be no public interest for such proceedings to take place; however, this statement was never fully explained. In the Supreme Court, in a short application of the rules of blasphemy, all the judges agreed with the judgment of Barrington J, as even though "it was impossible to say what the offence of blasphemy consisted of", he was able to say that it did not happen in this case. This was unusual as the corollary of saying what something is the ability to say what it is not. Therefore, the fact that Barrington J was able to state what did not constitute blasphemy would naturally suggest that he knew what blasphemy was.[115] However, this

---

[113] [2000] ILRM 426 and [1999] 4 IR 484.

[114] [1999] 4 IR 484 at 484.

[115] This point was also raised by Cox commenting on the *Corway* case, in "Case and Comment" (2000) 22 DULJ 201 at 205, stating that "First, the court concluded that it was unable to give definition to the crime of blasphemy, yet it had already referred to the definition given in *Murdoch's Dictionary of Irish Law*, without any suggestion that the definition therein offered was deficient. It is unclear why, having been cited with apparent approval it was then rejected. Secondly, the court was able to conclude that this particular cartoon was not blasphemous – a curious feat if the actus reus of the crime could not be defined."

was a unanimous decision in favour of the respondents and is now an extremely strong precedent for the future of the law of blasphemy in Ireland in its current state.

Since 1880, the ancient meaning of the word 'blasphemy' has been misused and the use of a "specific ancient term to cover a related modern problem is deeply problematic."[116] It has even caused some cynics to say "No one knows that blasphemy is ..., but all know what they are vague words which can be fitted to any meaning that shall please the ruling powers."[117]

Canon Law 2323 of the Roman Catholic Church is proffered for a definition of what blasphemy is. This states that "blasphemy is spoken or written words of insult to God or His Saints or sacred things".[118] This is further criticised by O'Higgins, stating that this definition does not include a breach of the peace and is irrelevant, unless the meaning of blasphemy in the Constitution has altered to the meaning proffered in Canon Law 2323.

It is important to consider the relevant provisions of the European Convention on Human Rights.[119] Article 10 of the European Convention of Human Rights allows for restrictions to be placed on freedom of expression for the "protection of health or morals"[120] and therefore, the right to freedom of expression "may be subject to such formalities, conditions, restrictions or penalties as are prescribed by law and are necessary in a democratic society".[121] In *Murphy v Ireland*,[122] the right of the applicant to place advertisements of a religious nature on national and local media was challenged in the Irish courts. Before the European Court of Human Rights, it turned on whether the interference was necessary. The court drew from the previous domestic court decisions that focused on the history of sectarian violence in Ireland and Northern Ireland. It stated "Irish people with religious beliefs tended to belong to a particular church so that religious advertising from a different church might be considered offensive and open to the interpretation of proselytism" and that "the very fact that an advertisement was directed towards a religious end which might

---

[116] N Cox, *Blasphemy and the Law in Ireland* (Edwin Mellen Press, Lewiston, New York, 2000), p 2.
[117] Quotation from W Bagehot as discussed in P O'Higgins, "Blasphemy in Irish Law" (1960) 23 Mod Law Rev 166.
[118] P O'Higgins, "Blasphemy in Irish Law" (1960) 23 Mod Law Rev 166, fn 82 at p 166.
[119] As part of the provisions of the European Convention of Human Rights Act 2003, the decisions of the Strasbourg Court have binding effect in Irish law.
[120] European Convention on Human Rights, Art 10(2).
[121] *ibid*, Art 10(2).
[122] (2004) 38 EHRR 212 and http://cmiskp.echr.coe.int/ (25 February 2007).

have been potentially offensive to the public".[123] On application of the margin of appreciation in Ireland's favour, the court stated that it:

> "agreed that the Government had been entitled to take the view that Irish citizens would resent having advertisements touching on these topics broadcast into their homes and that such an advertisement could lead to unrest".[124]

Regarding religious speech the most notable is the *Otto-Preminger-Institut* case.[125] There were to be six public showings of a satirical film on a religious subject matter. However, the film was seized and subsequently subject to a forfeiture order by the trial court. When the case was brought before the European Court of Human Rights, the Austrian government relied on the protection of Art 10(2), arguing this course of action was carried out to protect the rights of others. The court also stated that "[t]he demands of a democratic society mean that freedom of expression included the freedom to express ideas or to communicate information that shocks, offends or disturbs the state or any sector of the population".[126] The Defamation Act 2009 has laid down the statutory parameters for the new crime of blasphemy. Under s 36(2) of the Act, blasphemy is defined as follows:

> "He or she publishes or utters matter that is grossly abusive or insulting in relation to matters held sacred by any religion, thereby causing outrage amongst a substantial number of the adherents of that religion and he or she intends, by the publication or utterance of the matter concerned, to cause such outrage."[127]

However, it will be a defence if the defendant can prove that a reasonable person would find genuine literary, artistic, political, scientific, or academic value in the matter to which the offence relates.[128] The legislature specifically excludes any organisation or cult from the provisions of the legislation, by removing protection from any group which has a principal object of making money, or one which uses "oppressive psychological manipulation" of its followers, or in order to gain new followers.[129]

The introduction of the crime in the form of the Defamation Bill of

---

[123] *ibid*.
[124] *ibid*.
[125] *Otto–Preminger–Institut v Austria* [1995] 19 EHRR 34.
[126] *ibid* at 35.
[127] Defamation Act 2009, s 36(2).
[128] *ibid*, s 36(3).
[129] *ibid*, s 36(4).

2006 was surprising to many. The Bill had been on the legislative 'to do list' since its inception by the former Minister for Justice, Michael McDowell. It was only in April 2009 when the blasphemy provision was introduced. The blasphemy section was only read into the Bill during the Select Committee hearing. The constitutional reasons for including blasphemy into the Defamation Act could be explained with reference to the lack of an established religion in the country which was referenced in the *Corway* judgment. However, the Defamation Act also removed the offence of sedition which is also included as a constitutional offence in the free speech rights in the Constitution. Notwithstanding the incorporation of blasphemy within the Defamation Act, there is a proposed referendum on the retention or alteration of the constitutional crime of blasphemy.

### 7.6.4 Right to Assembly

The right to freedom of assembly is found in Art 40.6.1°(ii). The Constitution states that the "right of the citizens to assemble peaceably and without arms" is guaranteed. However, this right is restricted where such meetings are calculated to breach the peace or to be a danger or nuisance to the general public, and provision is made to prevent or control meetings in the vicinity of either House of the Oireachtas.

However, there are some additional restrictions on the right to assemble. If persons are trespassing on private property, then the meeting may not be considered an assembly capable of constitutional protections; the right to private property is also a protected constitutional right and as such assembly rights cannot override private property rights. If an assembly is causing a public nuisance, it is possible for an assembly on a roadway to be dispersed. As stated by Dicey, such lawful assemblies are for areas which comprise of common land which is left after everywhere else is considered. It is important to note that such rights are in the main shaped by Common Law principles. These are from the unwritten constitutional traditions of the United Kingdom. The general philosophy of Common Law rights is that a right to do something is what remains after everything else has been prohibited. This lack of clarity in unwritten constitutions shows the advantage of a written constitutional system, where rights are clearly stated in a positive nature, rather than sorting through case law to see what is prohibited to assess what is then granted to the subject, as in the United Kingdom.

A meeting which is not of a peaceable manner can be dispersed and those remaining may be charged under public order legislation for offences such as riot, violent disorder or affray. Under s 27 of the Offences against the State Act 1939, Gardaí are given statutory power to prohibit meetings in support of unlawful organisations. Under s 28 of the same Act, Gardaí are allowed to stop any public assembly within a half-mile of the Oireachtas or ask those to disperse. It has been stated that the section related to the Oireachtas may be unconstitutional as the provisions are overly broad. This means that there is a legitimate aim to the restriction, but the powers granted to regulate the assembly go beyond what is proportionate to the harm that may be caused. Also, the section does not make any reference to the nature of the assembly and yet the same power can be used by the Gardaí. The Criminal Justice (Public Order) Acts 1994 and 2003 also provide for the statutory regulation of assemblies and the organisation of such gatherings.

### 7.6.5 Right to Form Associations

The right to form associations impacts on the political life and work life of many citizens. The right to form associations grounds the right to form and partake in unions. This right is respected in many employment law provisions where, for example, a dismissal purely on the basis of union activity will be considered an automatic unfair dismissal. Also, when industrial action is sanctioned under the relevant legislation, members cannot be let go for being on strike. The text of Art 40.6.1°(iii) states that the right of citizens to form unions is recognised. However, laws may be enacted to regulate and control the exercise of the right in the public interest. For example, under the Offences against the State Acts, the membership of certain proscribed organisations is a criminal offence. This is due to the organisations in question seeking the violent overthrow of the state as terrorist organisations.

Citizens have a right to associate with a union or any other organisation. However, a union also has a right not to associate with an individual. In *Tierney v Amalgamated Society of Woodworkers*,[130] the society did not have to accept an apprentice as a member. It must also be noted that employment in an organisation does not mean that a person has to join a particular union. Also, employment in a workplace cannot be dependent on union status. In *Murphy v Stewart*,[131] it was held that the right to work in a particular place could not be reserved for members of a particular union. As with all rights in the Constitution, there is an implied right which is opposite to the express right. This is also the case with the right to association, a citizen also has the right not to be part of an organisation. For example, all students are charged a Union

---

[130] [1959] IR 254.
[131] [1973] IR 97.

of Students Ireland fee; however, a student is under no obligation to be a member of the union. In fact, many colleges have come and gone from the umbrella group and many individual students have left and returned to the Union of Students of Ireland. In *Meskell v CIÉ*,[132] the defendant company tried to sack all its workers with the opportunity of re-employment on the condition that they joined one of four recognised unions. The plaintiff refused this offer, stating that it was contrary to his right to dissociate. This was upheld by the Supreme Court.

Associations are not allowed to discriminate in the admittance of members. Under Art 40.6.2°, there is a prohibition on discrimination by associations on the basis of political, religious or class. This is also illustrated in the Employment Equality Acts 1998–2004 which prevent associations from discriminating against members. This would include representative associations and trade unions. Also, under equal status and equality law, an association cannot discriminate against a member or potential member on the basis of gender, age, marital status, sexual orientation, membership of the Traveller community, race or religion. Furthermore, unfair dismissals legislation will always consider a dismissal to be unfair if it results from a person's political membership or trade union membership. One of the most noteworthy cases on this point is *Portmarnock Golf Club v Ireland*.[133] This club would not extend full membership to women. Even though O'Higgins J in the High Court, by means of a case stated appeal, found in favour of the Club, he went on to give a full interpretation of the constitutional association issue. The club was found not to be discriminating due to the s 9 exemption where a club is providing for a specific need and not a general need, in this case the needs of male golfers. In the judgment of Higgins J, the use of single gender clubs did not infringe freedom of association but it was an issue to prevent the club from holding a liquor licence. However, the key observation was that freedom of association was subject to the restrictions stated in the Article itself, but this also implied the ground of equality which is also a personal right of the citizen. The case was subsequently appealed to the Supreme Court where the judgment of the High Court was upheld.

## 7.7 Family, Children and Education

The Constitutional rights in relation to the family are set out as a major part of the fundamental rights in the Constitution. The rights granted to the family impact on the rights to education as the family is considered to be the natural and primary educator of the child. Children's rights

---

[132] [1961] IR 345.
[133] [2005] IEHC 235.

are a relatively recent addition to the Constitution, following the referendum on the 31st Amendment of the Constitution in 2012. However, the inclusion of these rights was delayed by referendum petitions which challenged the mechanics of the referendum, so they were only incorporated into the text of the Constitution in 2015. The rights in the Constitution relating to the family, education and children are the foundation of family law.

### 7.7.1 Family Rights

The constitutional framing of the rights of the family can be interpreted as an important commentary on the construction of society as envisaged by the framers of the Constitution. The right of the family structure is stated in Art 41. The family was considered as the "natural and primary and fundamental unit group of Society".[134] This shows that the individual is not considered as the root of Irish society, as the family is considered as the "necessary basis for social order"[135] by the framers of the Constitution. The Article also considers the family to be "indispensable to the welfare of the Nation and the State".[136] It can also be argued that the traditional view of the family based upon marriage is wholly out of sync with the contemporary family units, but change is happening in this area, most recently with the successful marriage equality referendum.

natural law

Under Arts 41 and 42, the family rights are considered to be "inalienable and imprescriptible", which means that they cannot be given away and cannot be lost, and adhere to the natural law traditions in the Constitution.

The family is also considered to be a moral institution, and for this reason the family is considered to be primary education of the child. The rights of the family are considered to be "inalienable and imprescriptible rights" which are "antecedent and superior to all positive law". Under Art 41.2, the State guarantees to protect the family.

From *Murray v Ireland*,[137] that the rights are collective rights of the family and not individual rights of individual family members. The family as recognised by the Constitution is the one that is founded on marriage and not by genetic links. For example, in *State (Nicolaou)*

---

[134] Art 41.1.
[135] Art 41.2.
[136] Art 41.2 and should be read in conjunction with Art 41.2 regarding the life of the woman in the home.
[137] [1985] IR 532.

*v An Bord Uchtála*,[138] the right of an unmarried father to prevent the adoption of his biological child was not recognised, as he was not married to the mother of the child. This point was re-affirmed in *K v W*[139] and *W'OR v EH*.[140]

In *Mhic Mhathúna v Ireland*,[141] the court upheld the different treatment of one parent and two parent families under the social welfare system with regard to lone parent supports. It was held to be permissible as it recognised the extra financial burden on one parent families and such supports did not constitute an attack on the institution of marriage.

↳ *Reason pre-nups aren't allowed*

There are limits on the protection that will be afforded to families under constitutional law where the court has to balance the rights of the family against other rights in the common good. For example, in *Murray v Ireland*,[142] prison security considerations were significant enough to override prisoners' conjugal rights. In *Osheku v Ireland*,[143] family rights cannot be used to undermine immigration rules and family rights may be curtailed in the common good. The issue of immigration rules and the right to family, in particular the issue of Irish-born children, therefore Irish citizens, and the right to family life with their non-Irish or non-EU citizen parents was dealt with in *Lobe, Oysayande v Minister for Justice, Equality and Law Reform*,[144] where the court held that parents of non-EU citizens can be deported, even if it means that their Irish citizen children must effectively be deported with them.

↳ *Irish Citizens deported from Ireland.*

### 7.7.2 Marriage Equality

Prior to the 34th Amendment to the Constitution in 2015, marriage was not expressly defined in the constitution but interpreted through case law. In *Zappone & Anor v Revenue Commissioners & Others*[145] Dunne J stated that "marriage" under the terms of the Constitution is confined to couples of the opposite sex, as per the initial interpretation in *State (Nicolaou) v An Bord Uchtála*,[146] where the family was stated to be based on a married family. Marriage, until the introduction of the Marriage Act 2015, was a legal union between a man and a woman.

---

138 [1966] IR 567.
139 [1990] 2 IR 437.
140 [1996] 2 IR 248.
141 [1995] ILRM 69.
142 [1991] 1 ILRM 465.
143 [1987] ILRM 330.
144 [2003] 1 IR 1.
145 [2006] IEHC 404, [2008] 2 IR 417.
146 [1966] IR 567.

The Marriage Equality Referendum inserted Art 41.4 into the Constitution which states that "marriage may be contracted in accordance with law by two persons without distinction as to their sex".[147] The Marriage Act 2015 detailed the legislative procedures to expand on the constitutional provision but it also had the effect of removing the ability of either same sex couples to apply for civil partnership or to expand the ambit of civil partnerships to all couples regardless of gender.

### 7.7.3 The Status of Women

The provisions relating to the family contain the controversial provisions relating to a woman and her role within the home. Judging these provisions by the social conditions of today may not create a fair assessment of the considerations of the Irish Constitution for the equal role of women in society today. However, these Articles do provide an insight into the domestic role of women in the Ireland of 1937. The articles provided that "In particular, the State recognises that by her life within the home, woman gives to the State a support without which the common good cannot be achieved".[148] Article 41.2.2° further added to this provision by stating "The State shall, therefore, endeavour to ensure that mothers shall not be obliged by economic necessity to engage in labour to the neglect of their duties in the home."[149]

These articles have enraged equality activists and feminist activists since the time of their incorporation into the Constitution. The Articles were almost a policy reason to exclude married women from the civil and public service workforce up until the 1970s with the Marriage Bar that required married women to leave the civil sector. Under s 10(1) of the Civil Service Regulation Act 1956 women in the civil service were required to retire on marriage unless they were in an exempt position as declared by Minister for Finance. This was removed by the Civil Service (Employment of Married Women) Act 1973.

However, the provisions of the Articles have not received wide support in legal arguments in the courts for the protection of the family home or the provision of State supports to women in recognition of their duties in the home in cases such as L v L.[150] In that case, Barr J tried to use the provisions to provide homemakers with a beneficial interest in the family home, but it was overturned in the Supreme Court.[151]

---

[147] Art 41.4.
[148] Art 41.2.1°.
[149] Art 41.2.2°.
[150] [1989] ILRM 528.
[151] [1992] 2 IR 77.

There is a power of veto for the non-owning spouse to dealing with the family home under the Family Home Protection Act 1976, but it does not go as far as vesting a beneficial interest in the homemaker in respect of their work in the home. It is only since 1995 that homemakers who work in the home instead of the workforce have been recognised by the Social Welfare system by means of the provision of the homemaker's credit. The framing of the Articles also, by implication, devalues the work of men who choose to work at home. In 2013, the Constitutional Convention recommended the removal of these articles, and a referendum has been proposed on this issue.

### 7.7.4 Divorce

Considering the high value placed on the status of the family within the Constitution and noting the traditional Catholic values which run through Irish society, when the people eventually voted in favour of allowing divorce into their Irish legal system, the provisions were stated categorically in the Constitution to ensure that the criteria could not be amended without recourse to the people. The Constitution in Art 41.3.1° also states that "the State pledges itself to guard with special care the institute of Marriage, on which the Family is founded, and to protect it against attack". This ground was used to prevent discriminatory tax provisions against the family founded on marriage in *Murphy v Attorney General*.[152] The following section of the Constitution lays out the criteria for divorce in Art 41.2 where the spouses have lived apart from one another for a period or period amounting to four out of the previous five years, there is no reasonable prospect of reconciliation, financial provision has been made for spouses and children, and any further conditions prescribed by law.

The importance of placing the criteria for divorce into the Constitution was designed to allay fears of arbitrary changes to the time scales or any other relevant conditions by the Oireachtas. It was also a means of preventing any judicial activism regarding the grounds of divorce. Regarding the "living apart" requirement, the core element is mental separation or the "separate households" criteria. The courts and legislature have always regarded separate households as more important than physical separation. As one spouse may not have the financial means to seek separate accommodation, if it can be shown that both spouses maintained separate households over the specific time period, such as separate meal times, sleeping accommodation and living quarters, then this can fulfil the criteria without the need to "move out" of the family home, as shown in *McA v McA*.[153] The

---

[152] [1982] IR 241.
[153] [2000] 2 ILRM 48.

current time requirements for divorce of four out of five years living apart is proposed to be the subject of a referendum to reduce the period of time.

### 7.7.5 Education and the Constitution

The right to education is broadly outlined in Art 42. The concept of educator as stated in the Constitution is broader than the traditional association of education with schooling but extends to cover the complete formation of the child in terms of the "religious and moral, intellectual, physical and social education of their children".[154]

However, the State is only entitled to take the place of the parents through the social care system where there are exceptional circumstances. The criteria for such involvement has been broadened with the introduction of the rights of the child as independent to the parents in Art 42A. Where the parents are perceived to be failing in their duties to care for the "physical or moral" welfare of the child, then the State is entitled to take the place of the parents by means of care. The Child Care Act 1991 allows for the State to take children into care in emergency situations where the welfare of the child is under severe threat. The Adoption Act 1988 allows for marital children to be placed for adoption in such circumstances. However, due to the constitutional protection for the right of the parents, the use of such provisions only happen in the most extreme of circumstances. It is hoped that with the incorporation of the rights of the child into the Constitution that the sections above can be used in situations where there is an imminent danger to the life or well-being of the child but which would not have reached the high evidential threshold which was required before.

The Constitution recognises that the family is the primary and natural educator of the child.[155] The right is termed as being an inalienable right which correlates to the natural law basis of the constitutional rights. Parents are free to provide this education in their own homes, private schools or schools recognised or established by the State.[156] The State cannot make parents send their children to particular schools in violation of their conscience and lawful preference.[157] Where parents elect to educate their children at home, they must ensure that their children are receiving a suitable level of elementary education or the

---

[154] Art 42.1.
[155] Art 42.1.
[156] Art 42.2.
[157] Art 42.3.1°.

parents may be prosecuted as in *DPP v Best*.[158] This is also reflected in the provisions of Art 42.3.1° which allows for the State to ascertain that children are receiving a "certain minimum education, moral, intellectual and social".[159]

Under Art 42.4, the State will provide for free primary education and will support and give reasonable aid to private or educational corporate initiatives. Under the judgment of *Crowley v Ireland*,[160] it was established that this does not put an obligation on the State itself to provide education but to support and facilitate education in the State. The Article also gives parents a right in education with regard to the religious and moral formation of their children. In *Campaign to Separate Church and State v Minister for Education*,[161] the funding for school chaplains was constitutionally vindicated as it adhered to the right of parents to choice with regard to the religious and moral formation and education of their children.

The case of *Sinnott v Minister for Education*[162] demonstrated that the right to primary education expires once the child had reached the age of 18. This is based on the chronological age and not the mental age of the child; in *Sinnott* the child in question was 23 years old but had the intellectual age of a child due to a mental disability. The applicant sought extra resources to support her son. However, the case ultimately failed on the basis that the remedy sought would require financial assistance and the court would be unable to direct extra educational resources to the child, as this would be in violation of the doctrine of the separation of powers.

### 7.7.6 Children's Rights and the Constitution

As the Constitution considered that the rights of the family were superior to legislation, any variation with such rights would need to be carried out by means of a referendum. Also, it is important to realise that prior to the recent successful referendum, the rights of the child derived from the rights of the family. Children were not granted any rights independent of their parents. This meant that taking children into the care of social workers was close to impossible.

Even though Ireland was a signatory to international documents such as the UN Convention on the Rights of the Child, such instruments had no bearing on the children living in the Irish jurisdiction. This is

---

[158] [2000] 2 ILRM 1.
[159] Art 42.3.2°.
[160] [1980] IR 201.
[161] [1998] 2 ILRM 181.
[162] [2001] 2 IR 545.

because international agreements signed by the State have no bearing on the legal system until they are incorporated domestically, either by means of legislation or referendum under the terms of Art 29.

The 31st Amendment of the Constitution placed Art 42A into the Constitution. This Article provides for the protection of children independent of their position within the family. It "recognises and affirms the natural and imprescriptible rights of all children"[163] and creates rights with regard to the custody of children in social care settings[164] and in these proceedings the "best interests of the child shall be the paramount consideration."[165] The Article also enshrines the right of children to be heard and considering the maturity of the child.[166] Until the Article above is litigated in the courts, we will not know the full extent of the power of these children's rights and the degree to which the Article gives rights to children against the State or their parents.

## 7.8 Right to Property

The right to property is referenced in both Arts 40.3.2° where the personal rights of the citizen also mention the "property rights of every citizen" and the State will protect them "as best it may from unjust attack".[167] Article 43 contains the main enumerated rights to property in the Constitution.

The right to property is covered in Art 43. In Art 43.1.1° the State acknowledges the right to property in terms of a natural right to "private ownership of external goods".[168] Article 43.1.2° state that the State "guarantees to pass no law attempting to abolish the right of private ownership or the general right to transfer, bequeath, and inherit property".[169] However, as with all rights in the constitution, no right is absolute, and this is the case with the right to property. Article 43.2 creates limitations on the right in terms of the common good. Article 43.2.1° states that the State recognises that the rights in Art 43.1 must be

---

[163] Art 42A.1°.
[164] Art 42A.2.1° regarding placement in care, Art 42A.2.2° provides for the adoption of children of married parents in the best interests of the child and Art 42A.3 allows for the voluntary placement for adoption and adoption of any child.
[165] Art 42A.4.1°(iii).
[166] Art 42A.4.2°.
[167] Art 40.3.2°: "The State shall, in particular, by its laws protect as best it may from unjust attack and, in the case of injustice done, vindicate the life, person, good name, and property rights of every citizen."
[168] Art 43.1.1°.
[169] Art 43.1.2°.

regulated by the principles of social justice.[170] Article 43.2.2° states that the rights may be delimited by law "with a view to reconciling their exercise with the exigencies of the common good."[171] Interestingly, the courts have declined to interpret what is meant by "social justice". As per Hanna J in *Pigs Marketing Board v Donnelly (Dublin) Ltd*,[172] there was "no rule of law to guide the court" and the question was entirely one of "practical political science … a kind of political shibboleth, the meaning and application of which has changed and will continue to change from one generation to another".[173]

However, a workable example of social justice can be found in the legislation concerning the Dormant Accounts Fund. The dormant accounts fund was created by the Dormant Accounts Act 2001[174] which provides that money which is left in unclaimed or dormant accounts over a specified period can be used for social purposes where the account holder has been contacted and no action has been taken on the account. The fund is supervised by the Minister for Culture, Heritage and the Gaeltacht since July 2016. Even though this provision clearly infringes with an individual's right to property, it is line with the common good and principles of social justice as contained in Arts 43.2.1° and 43.2.2°.

Taxation, and its collection, could be considered to be an infringement on the right of a person to property. However, the collection of taxes is also in line with social justice and the common good. In *Madigan v Attorney General*,[175] O'Higgins CJ stated that the interference of taxation with the constitutional right to property

> "cannot be challenged as being unjust on that account, if what has been done can be regarded as action by the State in accordance with the principles of social justice and having regard to the exigencies of the common good as envisaged by Article 43.2."[176]

There are other examples of the right to property being limited in line with the common good. Where land is required for urban development or for the development of road and transport links, it is possible for

---

[170] Art 43.2.1°.
[171] Art 43.2.2°.
[172] [1939] IR 413.
[173] *ibid* at 418.
[174] See also the Unclaimed Life Assurance Policies Act 2003 and the Dormant Accounts (Amendment) Act 2012.
[175] [1986] ILRM 135.
[176] *ibid* at 161. However, the method used and the manner of calculation must be proportionate, as in *Heaney v Ireland* [1994] 3 IR 593.

the responsible State authority or local government area to issue compulsory purchase orders under the provisions of the Planning and Development Acts. There is a right to compensation for affected landowners in such situations; this would otherwise be regarded as an unjust attack on the constitutional rights of the property owner. In *Central Dublin Development Association v Attorney General*,[177] it was held that if land was to be acquired in such a fashion without the landowner receiving compensation, it would be an unjust attack. This point was also made by Keane CJ in *Re Article 26 and Part V of the Planning and Development Bill 1999*,[178] where adequate compensation was considered to be in line with at least the market value of the property that is to be compulsorily purchased in the interests of the common good. In *ESB v Gormley*,[179] even though the ESB was permitted to undertake work to run pylons through Gormleys' land without the landowner's permission there was still a requirement for the landowner to be compensated.

## 7.9 Religion and the Constitution

Religion, and its impact on the Constitution and constitutional rights, has already been noted in the discussion on freedom of expression in the Constitution.[180] The treatment of religion and its place within the Constitution is given a wider discussion in Art 44. The framing of religion in the Constitution heavily supports religious values, as in line with natural law traditions but it is subject to the principle of non-discrimination, which could arguably place it in the tradition of secular natural law as opposed to one with a theological foundation.

The 1922 Constitution was a "totally secular Constitution".[181] It did not give preference to one religion over another and the creators of that Constitution framed the rights of conscience, freedom of religion and freedom of expression in wide enough terms to cover the views of citizens of all religions and none. The tenets of one religion did not enjoy higher protection in law than the tenets of any other religion.[182]

Article 44, as originally drafted, recognised "the special position of the Catholic Apostolic and Roman Church as the guardian of the faith professed by the great majority of its citizens".[183] However, the original

---

[177] (1975) 109 ILTR 69.
[178] [2000] 2 IR 321.
[179] [1985] ILRM 494.
[180] See section 7.6.3.
[181] *Corway v Independent Newspapers* [1999] 4 IR 484 at 499.
[182] *ibid* at 499.
[183] JA Foley and S Lalor, *Gill & Macmillan Annotated Constitution of Ireland 1937–*

text of Bunreacht ná hÉireann recognised the Church of Ireland, the Presbyterian Church, the Methodist Church, the Religious Society of Friends and the Jewish Congregation and the other religions that existed in the State at the date of the coming into operation of the Constitution. The 5th Amendment sought to remove ss 2 and 3 of Art 44.1 which gave the Catholic Church its special position in the Irish Constitution and recognised the constitutional position of other named religions. It is important to note that during the time that this amendment was proposed, the general attitude was that this Article went too far in relation to creating a special position for the Catholic Church under Bunreacht ná hÉireann. However, a small minority of zealous Catholics felt that this Article did not go far enough. This group, which was called Maria Duce and led by Father Denis Fahy, complained that Art 44 only recognised the Catholic Church as the church of the majority, whereas they wanted the Catholic Church to be recognised "as the one true church founded by our Divine Lord".[184] In 1949, the organisation arranged a petition calling for an amendment of this article but the objections came to nothing, as there was no major political backing given to the organisation. Yet, less than thirty years later, the mores and ethos of the people had changed to such an extent that even Cardinal Conway, who was the Catholic Archbishop of Armagh and Primate of All Ireland stated that:

> "I personally would not shed a single tear if the relevant sub-section of Article 44 were to disappear. It confers no legal privilege whatsoever on the Catholic Church and, if the way to convince our fellow Christians in the North about this is to remove it, then it might be worth the expense of a referendum".[185]

The main argument behind the removal of this article was a contribution to removing the misconceptions held in the North and elsewhere about the nature of the Irish Republic.[186] Even though there was some opposition to the amendment, mainly from more conservative Catholic elements, the vote in favour of change was 84 percent. This was a significant result in relation to the changing attitudes of the Irish population. At the time that Bunreacht ná hÉireann was drafted, the Catholic Church in Ireland was in such an important position that Vatican approval had to be secured so that Bunreacht ná hÉireann would be passed. But now, its privileged position had declined to

---

1994: With Commentary (Gill & Macmillan, Dublin, 1995), p 128.
[184] Basil Chubb, The Constitution and Constitutional Change in Ireland (IPA, Dublin, 1978), p 62.
[185] ibid, p 68.
[186] ibid, p 69.

such a substantial degree that this constitutional position had now been removed.

It was never stated in the Irish Constitution that the Catholic Church was the established church of Ireland. The Anglican Church of Ireland which had been the established Church in Ireland was disestablished in 1869. Without doubt, it could be stated that the Roman Catholic Church is the majority church in Ireland. However, it must be remembered that it is not the established church in Ireland. Even Barrington J in the *Corway* case stated that "it was difficult to see how the common law crime of blasphemy could survive in a constitutional situation where there is no established church".[187] Also in the same case, Geoghegan J in the High Court hearing stated that:

> "I am satisfied, therefore, that in considering this application I need not concern myself with any particular words in the Constitution as either having the effect of expanding the meaning of blasphemy or as in some way superseding the common law offences."[188]

The current statement of religion in the Constitution acknowledges "the homage of public worship is due to Almighty God. It shall hold His Name in reverence, and shall respect and honour religion."[189] Additionally, Art 44.2 recognises "freedom of conscience and the free profession and practice of religion are, subject to public order and morality, guaranteed to every citizen".[190] The State will not "endow"[191] any religion; neither will it impose any "disabilities or make any discrimination on the ground of religious profession, belief or status".[192]

Considering the connection between education and religious orders, Art 44.2.4° states that financial assistance towards schools will not discriminate between different denominations. It is important in this regard to recall the right of parents to the moral education of their children and the right of parents to provide for the education of their children in this regard.[193] However, Art 44.2.4° also adds a freedom from religious instruction in these schools.[194]

---

[187] [2000] 1 ILRM 426 at 435.
[188] [1999] 4 IR 484 at 489.
[189] Art 44.1.
[190] Art 44.2.1°.
[191] Art 44.2.2°.
[192] Art 44.2.3°.
[193] Art 42.
[194] Art 44.2.4° which provides "Legislation providing State aid for schools shall not discriminate between schools under the management of different religious

The Constitution also makes provision for the administration of religious denominations and their right to manage their own affairs and property rights.[195] The property of religious denominations and any educational institution will not be diverted to other uses unless it is "necessary for necessary works of public utility and on payment of compensation",[196] which is similar to the general property rights in Art 43.

In spite of the principle of non-discrimination towards religious denominations, the State can fund religion in certain respects such as education and health care, once it is done in an even-handed manner, as in *Campaign to Separate Church and State v Minister for Education*.[197] Religious discrimination by the State is not permitted as in *M v An Bord Uchtála*,[198] where a provision of the Adoption Act 1952 prohibiting adoptions by couples of mixed religions was deemed unconstitutional.

However, it is important to note that there is still an allowable degree of discrimination on the grounds of religious ethos for staff working in religious-run educational institutions. In *Re Article 26 and the Employment Equality Bill 1996*,[199] the ability of certain training institutions and employers with a religious ethos to discriminate in recruitment and employment policies to preserve this ethos was subject to an Art 26 challenge. It was argued that such powers constituted an endowment of religion. The application failed and the court stated that such a provision did not:

> "involve the endowment of religion. The endowment of religion implies the selection of a favoured State religion for which permanent financial provision is made out of taxation or otherwise. This kind of endowment is outlawed (by this article of the Constitution)"[200]

In *Flynn v Power*,[201] the preservation of the religious ethos of a secondary school allowed for the dismissal of a teacher due to her being pregnant outside of marriage. Even though the dismissal was justified under

---

denominations, nor be such as to affect prejudicially the right of any child to attend a school receiving public money without attending religious instruction at that school."
[195] Art 44.2.5° which provides "Every religious denomination shall have the right to manage its own affairs, own, acquire and administer property, movable and immovable, and maintain institutions for religious or charitable purposes."
[196] Art 44.2.6°.
[197] [1998] 2 ILRM 181.
[198] [1975] IR 81.
[199] [1997] 2 IR 321.
[200] *ibid* at 354.
[201] [1985] IR 648.

the provisions of the Unfair Dismissals Act 1977, which predated the provisions of the Employment Equality Act, it was nonetheless permissible under the Act as it allowed for educational institutions to protect the religious ethos of the school and the provisions of the legislation were implied into her contract of employment.[202]

There is judicial support for the practice of religion as evident from the case of *Quinn's Supermarket v Attorney General*[203] which questioned the constitutionality of Sunday closing which allowed for exemptions for Jewish kosher shops. The Supreme Court held that in appropriate circumstances, such as in this case, religiously-motivated regulation that diverged from rules of general application could be upheld. In this instance, the ministerial order that allowed kosher shops to open on Sundays when all other shops were ordered to close was constitutional in order to facilitate Jewish observance of the Sabbath.

## 7.10 Socio-Economic Rights

The area of socio-economic rights is receiving increasing legal and academic attention. Socio-economic rights encompass social rights, such as the right to housing, healthcare and education, economic rights, such as the right to property, right to work and right to membership of a union, and cultural rights, such as a right to language, culture and religious expression. Traditionally, constitutional documents would only reflect the major civil and political rights, as the Constitution was regarded as a political document. However, the Irish Constitution included a number of these socio-economic rights, such as property rights and language rights. The right to civil and political life, and personal rights could be considered to be cross-cutting rights which allow for socio-economic rights to be perused.

This was recently one of the core areas for consideration by the Constitutional Convention in its deliberations. The question that was put to the members of the Convention was whether there should be a greater role for such socio-economic rights in the Constitution in the future. Furthermore, issues such as direct provision for refugees, the homelessness crisis, and the issues in healthcare provision, be it access to medication or access to facilities, has caused civil society to look more closely at the rights that are in the Constitution to see if these

---

[202] *ibid* at 657 as per Costello J "In the present case, the appellant knew from her own upbringing and previous experience as a teacher the sort of school in which she sought employment, and should have been well aware of the obligations she would undertake by joining its staff."

[203] [1972] IR 1.

socio-economic rights can be used as a means of accessing services or seeking reforms to State services.

### 7.10.1 Directive Principles of Social Policy

Hogan and Whyte state that the directive principles of social policy are influenced from Roman Catholic social teaching which pursues a philosophy of communitarianism which seeks to promote the common good.[204] Article 45 lists principles of social policy that are for the general guidance of the Oireachtas in the creation of legislation.[205] Even though this Article follows the fundamental rights section of the Constitution and the contents of the Article could be read like rights, the courts have not used them individually to ground rights as per the limitation set out in the opening section of Art 45. Furthermore, the separation of powers[206] is an issue with any use of the directive principles as they are for the application of the Oireacthas in the creation of legislation and not for the court to use as means of enforcing these principles.

The Article lists a number of issues that the Oireachtas must take into account when creating legislation. The first principle is that the State "shall strive to promote the welfare of the whole people by securing and protecting as effectively as it may a social order in which justice and charity shall inform all the institutions of the national life."[207] The invocation of the concepts of "justice" and "charity" resonates with the general tenor of natural law and rights grounded on such jurisprudence. Article 45.2 requires the State to direct policies that the Oireachtas is making into law towards securing the following ends:

> "i That the citizens (all of whom, men and women equally, have the right to an adequate means of livelihood) may through their occupations find the means of making reasonable provision for their domestic needs.[208]
>
> ii That the ownership and control of the material resources of the community may be so distributed amongst private

---

[204] G Hogan and G Whyte, *JM Kelly: The Irish Constitution* (4th ed, Tottel Publishing, Dublin, 2006), p 2079.

[205] Art 45: "The principles of social policy set forth in this Article are intended for the general guidance of the Oireachtas. The application of those principles in the making of laws shall be the care of the Oireachtas exclusively, and shall not be cognisable by any Court under any of the provisions of this Constitution."

[206] See the discussion on the separation of powers in 5.1.

[207] Art 45.1.

[208] See *Tierney v Amalgamated Society of Woodworkers* [1959] IR 254 (discussed in section 7.6.5), where the provisions of this Article were used as a means of interpretation to create a right to livelihood and the judicial interpretation of the directive principles of social policy (discussed in section 7.10.2).

individuals and the various classes as best to subserve the common good.

iii That, especially, the operation of free competition shall not be allowed so to develop as to result in the concentration of commodities in a few individuals to the common detriment.

iv That in what pertains to the control of credit the constant and predominant aim shall be the welfare of the people as a whole.

v That there may be established on the land in economic security as many families as in the circumstances shall be practicable."

The directive principles of social policy also include private industry in the consideration of the achievement of common good in Art 45.3. Article 45.3.1° states that the State shall "favour and, where necessary, supplement private initiative in industry and commerce."[209] However, the degree of such supplementation that is now permissible since Ireland joined the EU with its regulations and rules on State aid of private industry means that, even with the limited used of the directive principles of social policy, such aid could be deemed contrary to EU law. Article 45.3.2° is highly economic in nature and states that the

"State shall endeavour to secure that private enterprise shall be so conducted as to ensure reasonable efficiency in the production and distribution of goods and as to protect the public against unjust exploitation."[210]

Again, this statement on the regulatory philosophy of private industry and commerce in the State reflects the ideal of communitarianism and seeks to direct the Oireachtas to regulate business in line with the common good. The tenor of the directive principles of social policy with regard to economic issues was used in *Kerry Co-Operative Creameries v An Bord Bainne*[211] as a means for interpreting the common law doctrine of restraint of trade.

The final article dealing with the directive principles of social policy looks towards the weaker in society. In Art 45.4.1°, the State, through the directives, pledges "to safeguard with especial care the economic

---

[209] Art 45.3.1°.
[210] Art 45.3.2°.
[211] [1991] ILRM 851.

interests of the weaker sections of the community, and, where necessary, to contribute to the support of the infirm, the widow, the orphan, and the aged."[212] The State, through the directives will

> "endeavour to ensure that the strength and health of workers, men and women, and the tender age of children shall not be abused and that citizens shall not be forced by economic necessity to enter avocations unsuited to their sex, age or strength."[213]

This point was taken in *Landers v Attorney General*[214] as a means to interpret the regulations concerning child labour and the court considered the directive principles of social policy in considering the constitutionality of pre-1937 legislation.

### 7.10.2 Judicial Interpretation of Socio–Economic Rights

In *Murtagh Properties v Cleary*,[215] *Tierney v Amalgamated Society of Woodworkers*,[216] and *Landers v Attorney General*[217] (amongst others), the provisions of Art 45 were used as an interpretive tool to assess the principles behind the legislation in question. Particularly in *Murtagh Properties*, Kenny J stated that the use of Art 45 as a directive to the Oireachtas did not "involve the conclusion that the courts may not take it into consideration when deciding whether a claimed constitutional right exists".[218]

In *TD v Ireland*,[219] a hard line view on the use of the directive principles of social policy was taken by the Supreme Court as follows:

> "With the exception of Article 42 of the Constitution, under the heading 'Education', there are no express provisions therein cognisable by the courts which impose an express obligation on the State to provide accommodation, medical treatment, welfare or any other form of socio-economic benefit for any of its citizens, however needy or deserving."[220]

---

[212] Art 45.4.1°.
[213] Art 45.4.2°.
[214] (1975) 109 ILTR 1.
[215] [1972] IR 330.
[216] 1959] IR 254.
[217] (1975) 109 ILTR 1.
[218] [1972] IR 330 at 336.
[219] [2001] 4 IR 259.
[220] *ibid* at 316.

However, this hard line statement of the use and interpretation of socio-economic rights into the constitution has somewhat softened. *Re Article 26 of the Constitution and the Health (Amendment) (No. 2) Bill, 2004*,[221] concerned an Art 26 reference of legislation which sought to retrospectively validate charges for hospitals and nursing homes which were found to be unlawfully levied on medical card holders. Speaking for the court, Murray CJ stated

> "It seems to the Court that it cannot be gainsaid, having regard to its well established jurisprudence, that it is for the Oireachtas in the first instance to determine the means and policies by which rights should be respected or vindicated. Counsel assigned by the Court are correct in submitting that the doctrine of the separation of powers, involving as it does respect for the powers of the various organs of State and specifically the power of the Oireachtas to make decisions on the allocation of resources, cannot in itself be a justification for the failure of the State to protect or vindicate a constitutional right".[222]

In the more recent cases to actually develop the concept of socio-economic rights, the courts have been more willing to read such rights through the Constitution as in *O'Donnell v South Dublin County Council*[223] where a right to suitable temporary accommodation for a disabled Traveller was upheld.

It is also important to note the decision in *Merriman v Fingal County Council*,[224] where Barrett J specifically references the wellbeing of citizens which could be argued to constitute a social right in line with the common good:

> "Along with legislative change, and well within the lifetime of this Court, there has also surfaced (i) a rising public concern about increasing environmental degradation and (ii) a greater public awareness that the quality of our life as a nation, and as members of the wider human community, is threatened by the processes which have yielded the very quality of life which we presently enjoy. It is in this, not un-pressing, context that the Case 2 (Friend of the Irish Environment) Applicant contends that there resides

---

[221] [2005] IESC 7.

[222] *ibid*.

[223] Specifically, in the High Court judgment [2008] IEHC 454, and also in the Supreme Court judgment [2015] IESC 28.

[224] [2017] IEHC 695.

within the Constitution an unenumerated and previously not expressly recognised personal right to an environment that is consistent with the human dignity and well-being of citizens at large."

However, it is important to note O'Dell's commentary on the issue stating that there is a

Journal
Article →

"very significant difference between asking a court to grant a mandatory injunction directing the State to protect a socio-economic interest in the absence of any legislation, as was the case in Sinnott and TD, and inviting a court, as in the instant case, to review legislation that affects such an interest."[225]

### 7.10.3 Reform Recommendations for Socio-Economic Rights

The Constitutional Review Group in 1996, on consideration of the directive principles of social policy was divided on their retention, but stated that if they were to be retained, then it should also cover the government as well as the Oireachtas and adding that if they were to be retained, further principles to "reflect modern concerns in regard to socioeconomic rights"[226] should be added to the article.

The Eighth Report of the Constitutional Convention specifically addresses its considerations on the constitutional recognition of socio-economic rights.[227] Eighty-five percent of the members voted to strengthen the protection of economic, social and cultural rights in the Constitution. There was majority support for making recommendations at the time of the report to insert a provision into the constitution that "the State shall progressively realise ESC rights, subject to maximum available resources and that this duty is cognisable by the Courts",[228] thereby amending the current framework for the directive principles of social policy in the constitution to make them applicable before the courts, which would increase their legal effect from just guidelines to

---

[225] E O'Dell "Is This a Country for Old Men and Women? In re Article 26 and the Health (Amendment) (No.2) Bill 2004" (2005) 27 DULJ 368 at 371.

[226] *Report of the Constitution Review Group* (July 1996), available at http://archive. constitution.ie/reports/crg.pdf (accessed 8 January 2018).

[227] *Eighth Report of the Convention on the Constitution–Economic, Social and Cultural (ESC) Rights* (March 2014), available at https://www.constitution. ie/AttachmentDownload.ashx?mid=5333bbe7-a9b8-e311-a7ce-005056a32ee4 (accessed 8 January 2018).

[228] *Eighth Report of the Convention on the Constitution–Economic, Social and Cultural (ESC) Rights* (March 2014), p 6, available at https://www.constitution.ie/ AttachmentDownload.ashx?mid=5333bbe7-a9b8-e311-a7ce-005056a32ee4 (accessed 8 January 2018).

the Oireachtas in carrying out their legislative duties. The Convention's Report recommended that there should be additional rights placed in the Constitution for housing, essential health care, rights of people with disabilities, linguistic and cultural rights and also rights covered in the International Covenant on Economic, Social and Cultural Rights.[229] All of these grounds were supported by between 78 percent and 90 percent of the Convention members.[230]

[229] ibid.
[230] ibid.

# CHAPTER EIGHT

# AMENDING, INTERPRETING AND REVIEWING THE CONSTITUTION

## 8.0 Introduction

As the constitution acts as the primary legal source for the Irish jurisdiction is necessary for the text to be either changed or interpreted by the courts through judicial review. The Constitution includes provisions for the holding of referendums to allow for articles to be amended, replaced or expanded by means of popular vote. The constitution may also be interpreted by the courts to see what is meant by the provisions that are stated in the document. Recently there has been a growing move to convene bodies to examine the need for Constitutional change and proposed amendments to be made by means of referendum. This chapter will explore these mechanisms.

## 8.1 Amending the Constitution

The amendment of the Constitution is carried out by means of referendum. The word referendum can relate to both an ordinary referendum and a constitutional referendum. The general scheme of provisions to amend the Constitution is set out in Arts 46 and 47 of the Constitution. Unlike the previous 1922 Constitution, it was possible to amend any article of the Constitution bar these provisions for a period of five years from its enactment.[1]

Since the coming into operation of the Constitution, there have been 33 amendments to the Constitution. Thirty-one of these amendments have been voted on by the electorate. The first amendment of the Constitution in 1939 covered the emergency provisions which were put in place during the Second World War in which Ireland was not a participant, but the provisions were required to protect public safety. The second amendment in 1941 was to tidy up various articles of the Constitution in light of its enactment. Neither amendment required a referendum, as they were carried out during the five-year transitory period. Since then, at least 34 referendums have been carried out on areas such as divorce, marriage equality, the removal of the special position of the Catholic Church, and various EU treaty enactments. Many more referendums are planned on such issues as abortion, blasphemy, the constitutional position of women in the home, and likely more EU treaty enactments.

### 8.1.1 The Amendment Process in the Oireachtas

The general process for the amendment of the Constitution is detailed in Art 46. All amendments have to follow the procedures laid down in

---

[1] See the historical background to the Constitution in chapter 2 for a further elaboration on the 1922 Constitution.

the article and must be started in the Dáil as a Bill and passed by both Houses of the Oireachtas. The process of a Constitutional amendment is similar to the legislative process of ordinary legislation, except that the people must assent to the proposal by vote before the President is entitled to sign off on the change.[2] Any proposal to amend the Constitution must be started in the Dáil as a Bill. The Bill must be titled as "An Act to amend the Constitution". The Bill must either pass the Seanad by majority or it will be deemed to have been passed by the Seanad.[3] There can only be one proposal in each Bill to amend the Constitution. Due to the costs involved in holding a referendum, it is common for more than one proposal to be put before the people on one day. However, in spite of the financial advantages of running more than one vote on one day, it does mean that some referendum proposals receive more publicity than other votes on the same day. An example of this would be the 34th Amendment to the Constitution on marriage equality referendum. This was a high-profile referendum and overshadowed the failed 35th Amendment to the Constitution to reduce the minimum age for candidacy for the office of President from 35 years to 21 years. Further, any media coverage of referendums has to be balanced, so there must be an equal weight of arguments both for and against the proposed referendum. This means that where there is a small number of people lobbying either for or against the measure, the amount of debate is limited.[4]

### 8.1.2 The Voting Procedure

The process for the referendum itself is set out in Art 47 of the Constitution. Citizens who are entitled to vote in Dáil elections are entitled to vote on constitutional referendums. You must be registered to vote in order to be able to cast your vote on such issues. Remember that there are different categories of voters in the Irish system. Only Irish citizens are entitled to vote in all referendums, as well as in presidential, Dáil, local, and EU elections. UK nationals who are resident in Ireland are entitled to vote in Dáil, local and EU elections. European citizens are entitled to vote in local and European elections only. Non-EU citizens are entitled to vote in local elections.

In order for a constitutional referendum to be passed, a majority of votes cast must be in favour of the proposed amendment. For constitutional referendums, there is no "quorum" of votes necessary.

---

[2]  See the legislative process as detailed in section 5.2.3 dealing with the organs of government.
[3]  Where the Seanad votes against a proposal to amend the Constitution, the Bill will be deemed to have passed after 180 days under the provisions of Art 23.1.
[4]  See the section on freedom of expression at 7.6.1 and the section on equality at 7.4.

However, for ordinary referendums, one-third of the electors on the register must cast their vote. An ordinary referendum transpires when the President exercises his power under Art 27[5] to refuse to sign a Bill until the people have had their chance to give their opinion on a matter of national importance. It should be noted that to this date, no such referendum has taken place.

It is also important to bear in mind that the provisions of Art 47 only deal with the broad issues of the referendum process. The process is also governed by the Referendum Act 1994 which sets out the legislative framework for the management of the referendum process, such as expenses in referendums, ballot secrecy, the conduct of the election, the counting of votes and the use of referendum petitions to challenge the referendum result on the basis of a material defect with the process. Also the Referendum Act 1998 established the Referendum Commission on an ad hoc basis to ensure the dissemination of balanced information on the proposed referendum. This Commission was established in the wake of the *McKenna*[6] case.

### 8.1.3 Challenging and Finishing the Process

Where a referendum takes place and the votes are counted, the referendum Returning Officer will issue a provisional certificate of the referendum result under s 40 of the Referendum Act 1994. If no objection has been received by the High Court within seven days of the issuing of the provisional certificate of the result, then the certificate becomes final and the Bill is then signed into law. There have been occasions where the result of a referendum has been challenged but none have been successful.

Both the results of the divorce referendum and the children's rights referendum were challenged unsuccessfully on the basis that the information given by the government in breach of the precedent set down in McKenna[7] affected the legitimacy of the referendum result. In *Hanafin v Minister for the Environment*,[8] the court upheld the result in the divorce referendum even though it had been previously found that the government had exceeded its role in the referendum with regard to the information supplied to the voters. Similarly, in *Jordan v Minister for Children and Youth Affairs*,[9] the information campaign by the government was previously found to have exceeded the powers of

---

[5]   This article and the powers of the President in relation to legislation will be dealt with later.
[6]   *McKenna v An Taoiseach (No.1)* [1995] 2 IR 1.
[7]   *ibid.*
[8]   [1996] 2 IR 321.
[9]   [2015] IESC 33.

government in a referendum,[10] but again it was not held to invalidate the result of the referendum. For a referendum petition it must be demonstrated that there was a material defect in the process of holding a referendum and government information campaigns, even though they transgress the constitutional role of government, are not enough to be held as a material defect in the referendum process.[11]

### 8.1.4 The Referendum Commission

In the *McKenna (No.2)* case, the Supreme Court ruled that it was unconstitutional for the government to use State monies for the communication or promotion of a particular side in a constitutional referendum. The only role of the State was in providing the machinery for the holding of a referendum. They did make a distinction between parties and the government. O'Flaherty J stated that:

> "The public purse must not be expended to espouse a point of view which may be anathema to certain citizens who, of necessity, have contributed to it … I should think it bordering on the self-evident that in a democracy such as is enshrined in our Constitution (which is not exclusively a parliamentary democracy; it has element of a plebiscitary democracy) it is impermissible for the Government to spend public money in the course of a referendum campaign to benefit one side rather than the other."[12]

In the wake of this decision, the government set up the Referendum Commission in order to publicise the holding of a referendum and the issue to be addressed. The Commission was established by the Referendum Act 1998, and this was subsequently amended by the Referendum Act 2001.

### 8.1.5 Upcoming Referendums

A number of proposed referendum questions are to be put to the people between May 2018 and June 2019. The referendum on repealing the 8th amendment is scheduled to take place on 25 May 2018 which will entail the removal of Art 40.3.3°.[13] October 2018 should see referendums on blasphemy in the Constitution, the amendment of the Article relating to the position of women in the home and the creation

---

[10] *McCrystal v The Minister for Children and Youth Affairs* [2012] 2 IR 726.

[11] For an example of what is a material defect, *Kiely v Kerry County Council* [2015] IESC 97 can be used as an example from Electoral Law where a defect in the count process was held to be a material defect.

[12] *McKenna v An Taoiseach (No.1)* [1995] 2 IR 1 at 43.

[13] See the consideration of the right to life in section 7.5.

of directly-elected mayors. These referendums should coincide with the Presidential election that may be held if candidates declare against President Michael D Higgins seeking another term of office. The last tranche of referendums will be held to coincide with the local and European elections in June 2019. These referendums will be on the reduction of the waiting periods for divorce from four to two years, the reduction of the voting age from 18 to 16 and the extension of voting rights to emigrants.

## 8.2 Constitutional Interpretation

Even with the mechanism of the referendum as outlined in Arts 46 and 47 of the Constitution, it is still open to the courts to interpret the Constitution. This may even result in changing the nuances of the interpretation of the text without changing the actual document. This point was made in the case of *McGee v Attorney General*,[14] where the court conceded that the Constitution must be interpreted in line with the prevailing ideas of the time in order to be consistent with the common good.

### 8.2.1 Interpreting the Constitution

Even though the Constitution is written in a straightforward manner in comparison to other legal documents, there are still times when a court must consider what is meant by an article or subsection. Only the courts may make an adjudication on the interpretation of an Article, although many arguments are made by lawyers and academics. In order to assess the meaning of an Article or phrase, certain rules of construction are used. There are many rules used by the courts when interpreting the Constitution, but this section will consider the main rules used. In many instances, these rules are similar to their counterparts used in interpreting legislation. The concept of stare decisis also holds in the interpretation of the Constitution, in that the precedents set by the Supreme Court bind the High Court. The precedents of the Supreme Court can be changed but only where there is an overwhelming reason to do so, as was set in *State (Quinn) v Ryan*.[15] However, the court must strike a balance between keeping the Constitution relevant to prevailing social conditions and the need for certainty in the application of precedent.

---

[14] [1974] IR 284.
[15] [1965] IR 70 echoing the judgment in *Attorney General v Ryan's Car Hire* [1965] 1 IR 64.

### 8.2.2 The Literal Approach

The literal approach is where the ordinary everyday meaning is attributed to words. In *DPP v O'Shea*,[16] the Supreme Court was asked to adjudicate on the meaning of Art 34.4.3°, which provided for a right to appeal to the court following any decision of the High Court or other courts prescribed by law. In this case, the appeal of a decision from the Central Criminal Court to the Supreme Court was questioned. As the Central Criminal Court was established by law, it followed that the provisions of Art 34.4.3° could be used to allow for a hearing of the argument in the Supreme Court as this was what was literally meant by the Article in question.[17]

### 8.2.3 The Purposive Approach

The purposive approach, which is also known as the broad approach, looks at the totality of the Constitution on an issue in order to establish the essence of the meaning. The purposive approach is focused on reading the Constitution in light of its aims and purposes. In *Maguire v Ardagh*,[18] Keane CJ stated that the "constitution is a political charter, using the adjective in its broadest sense. One does not expect to find in it the level of detail which, in our legislative traditions, we associate with Acts, regulations and by-laws". In *Attorney General v Paperlink*,[19] the question before the court was whether the Constitution, notwithstanding the political right to communicate convictions and opinions as found in Art 40.6.1°(i), also included a general right to communicate. As the construction of Art 40.6.1°(i) referred to the political activities of the right to freedom of expression, relief could also be found in the personal rights of the citizen as contained in Art 40.3.1°, the unenumerated rights article, so the court was able to ground a general right to communicate in the personal rights.[20]

### 8.2.4 The Harmonious Approach

The harmonious approach looks at different parts of the Constitution, as they should not be read in isolation. For example, if one was to define democracy in terms of the Irish Constitution it would not be sufficient to look at only one article of the Constitution when many

---

[16]  [1982] IR 384.
[17]  This right of appeal has now been altered with the provision of the Court of Criminal Appeal and the removal of the right to appeal to the Supreme Court by s 11 Criminal Procedure Act 1993. There is still a right of final appeal on a constitutional question to the Supreme Court after the appeal has passed through the Court of Criminal Appeal.
[18]  [2002] 2 IR 385.
[19]  [1984] ILRM 373.
[20]  See further section 7.6.1 on the right to freedom of expression.

articles touch on the democratic structures of the State. In the case above, this approach was summarised by O'Higgins CJ[21] by stating that the Constitution must be looked at as a whole and not merely in parts and that if ambiguity exists, other sections should be consulted to see if they can enhance the meaning. For example, in *Doherty v Referendum Commission*,[22] Hogan J considered the link between the role of the citizen under Art 6.1 and the construction of Art 40.6.1°. Hogan J stated that the nature of Art 6.1 created the form of popular sovereignty where citizen were to be called on to make "critical decisions",[23] that Art 40.6.1° envisaged "informed citizenry",[24] and where referendums encouraged the citizens to "engage in robust political debate so that the forces of deliberation will prevail over the arbitrary and irrational so that, in this civic democracy, reasoned argument would prevail in this triumph of discourse".[25] It was also stated that under the provisions of Art 9.3 that the Constitution placed a "premium on honest and fearless debate"[26] in times of referendums. As can be seen in this case, there were many other articles considered when adjudicating the interpretation of a single right.

### 8.2.5 The Historical Approach

In order for constitutions to remain relevant to current society, it is necessary to reinterpret their provisions. However, in some instances regard will be had to the considerations of the framers of the constitution. It could be argued that this approach is controversial. This is clear from the contrasts between the cases of *Zappone & Anor* and the *McGee* case.

In *McGee v Attorney General*,[27] the right to marital privacy, particularly the right to access contraceptives, was at issue. In this case, a married couple was prevented from accessing contraception. They claimed that their marital privacy was invaded when an illegal consignment was stopped by customs. At the time, the sale and supply of contraceptives was illegal. Mrs McGee was told that she would be putting her life in jeopardy if she were to become pregnant again. The court ruled that this prohibition infringed the privacy of a married couple. The High Court held that the right to marital privacy would not have been accepted by those who wrote the 1937 Constitution and thereby no such right existed. However, the Supreme Court overturned this

---

21  *DPP v O'Shea* [1982] IR 384.
22  [2012] IEHC 211.
23  *ibid* at para 21.
24  *ibid* at para 24.
25  *ibid* at para 23.
26  *ibid* at para 22.
27  [1974] IR 284.

decision on the basis that no constitution could be intended to be final for all time, but must change in light of prevailing ideas and concepts.

In *Zappone & Anor v Revenue Commissioners & Others*,[28] the plaintiffs were a same sex couple who were married under the law of another country. Heterosexual foreign marriages are recognised under Irish law. The argument centred on the treatment of their legal marriage under Irish taxation law, arguing that the non-recognition of their married status was discriminatory. In this case, the High Court did apply the historical approach stating that society had not changed to such an extent that there was consensus to change the historical meaning of marriage in the Irish Constitution to that which included same sex marriage, or the acceptance of marriage equality.

Both cases highlight a tension between the application and non-application of the historical approach. It could be argued that if societal change is to be reflected in the Constitution that it should be done by referendum, as such change may be argued to be more of a change to the nature of the Constitution itself rather than an interpretation.

### 8.2.6 The Natural Law Approach

Natural law theory is based on the philosophical understanding that there are certain rights to which a person is entitled as they are inherent in their nature. For example, the right to life is considered to be a natural law right as it is common to all humans and derived from nature. Natural law rights are different from positive law rights. Positive law is considered as man-made law. Such a natural law approach is clear from the Catholic ethos enshrined in the Preamble which states:

> "In the Name of the Most Holy Trinity, from Whom is all authority and to Whom, as our final end, all actions of both men and States must be referred."

Even though the Preamble is not a legally binding part of the Constitution, this opening paragraph acts as a lens and frame for the interpretation of the Constitution. In the late 1930s, Ireland was a predominately Catholic country. Even a draft copy of the Constitution was sent to the Vatican for consideration.[29] However, this natural law emphasis on constitutional rights cannot be used to undermine legislation which is the result of a referendum. For example, in *Re*

---

[28]  [2006] IEHC 404, [2008] 2 IR 417.
[29]  It must be noted that a referendum in 1972 removed the special position of the Catholic Church.

*Article 26 and Regulation of Information (Services Outside of the State for the Termination of Pregnancies) Bill,*[30] the court had to assess whether the Bill was constitutional in spite of the legislation resulting from the passing of the 14th Amendment to the Constitution. This amendment was to allow for the dissemination of information on abortion services outside of the State, notwithstanding the constitutional prohibition on abortion in the State.

Prior to the referendum, the right to life of the unborn child was recognised by the Constitution through the natural law interpretation of the Constitution and the insertion of the 8th Amendment, which recognised the equal right to life of the mother and the unborn child, and particularly through the judgment of *The Attorney General (S.P.U.C.) v Open Door Counselling Ltd*[31] and reaffirmed in *S.P.U.C. v Grogan.*[32] Referring to the ability of the citizens to amend the constitution by referendum and the link with natural law, Hamilton CJ stated the following:

> "It is fundamental to this argument that, what is described as 'the natural law' is the fundamental law of this State and as such is antecedent and superior to all positive law, including the Constitution and that it is impermissible for the People to exercise the power of amendment of the Constitution by way of variation, addition or repeal, as permitted by Article 46 of the Constitution unless such amendment is compatible with the natural law and existing provisions of the Constitution and, if they purport to do so, such amendment had no effect.
>
> The Court does not accept this argument."[33]

Therefore, once an amendment is passed by the citizens through referendum, no pre-existing interpretation of the Constitution may be used to undermine the will of the people.

### 8.2.7 Presumption of Constitutionality

Article 15.4 of the Constitution clearly establishes the presumption of constitutionality of legislation as follows:

> "1° The Oireachtas shall not enact any law which is in any

---

[30] [1995] 1 IR 1.
[31] [1988] IR 593.
[32] [1989] IR 753.
[33] [1995] 1 IR 1 at 38.

respect repugnant to this Constitution or any provision thereof.

2° Every law enacted by the Oireachtas which is in any respect repugnant to this Constitution or to any provision thereof, shall, but to the extent only of such repugnancy, be invalid."

Therefore, any legislation passed by the Oireachtas will be deemed to be in accordance with the provisions of the Constitution. It also means that the Oireachtas must be mindful of the provisions of the Constitution when considering any Bills before it. This provision was used as a means to block the Protection of Life in Pregnancy (Amendment) (Fatal Foetal Abnormalities) Bill 2013 by a Dáil vote, as it was argued in the Dáil that the legislation was unconstitutional.

Even legislation that has successfully been promulgated into law may still have a constitutional defect. If the defect only relates to one section of the legislation, then only that section will be deemed to be unconstitutional. However, if the defect spans the entire legislation, then the entirety of the act will cease to have effect. An example of a recent case where legislation was found to be unconstitutional was *Bederev v Ireland*.[34] In the Court of Appeal judgment,[35] it was found that s 2(2) of the Misuse of Drugs Act gave the government law-making powers, which powers are the domain of the Oireachtas. However, on appeal to the Supreme Court, a unanimous seven judge panel found that there were sufficient safeguards in the legislation, so s 2(2) of the Act was found constitutional.[36]

Even though legislation may have the presumption of constitutionality, there may be instances where the defect in the legislation is so obviously unconstitutional that the presumption of constitutionality is very easy to rebut. This was the case in *M v An Bord Uchtála*,[37] where s 12(1) of the Adoption Act 1952 precluded adoptions to couples of

---

[34]  [2016] IESC 34.

[35]  [2015] IECA 38.

[36]  For a full list of cases where legislation was deemed to be unconstitutional, see G Hogan, D Kenny and R Walsh, "An Anthology of Declarations of Unconstitutionality" (2015) 54(2) *Irish Jurist* 1–30.

[37]  [1975] 1 IR 81. At the time of the legislation, the old version of Arts 44.1.2° and 44.1.3° were in force which recognised the Catholic Church, Church of Ireland, the Presbyterian Church in Ireland, the Methodist Church in Ireland, the Religious Society of Friends in Ireland, as well as the Jewish Congregations and the other religious denominations. The 5th Amendment of the Constitution was passed in 1972 which replaced these articles and in Art 44.2.1° establishes freedom of conscience and the free profession and practice of religion guaranteed to every citizen.

mixed religions. This legislation had surprisingly passed the legislative process even though it was completely inconsistent with the freedom of religion.

### 8.2.8 Double Construction

Where provisions of legislation may have two different interpretations, one which renders the legislation unconstitutional and the other that preserves the constitutionality of the legislation, the interpretation which preserves the constitutionality of the provisions will be preferred. This is linked to the presumption of constitutionality. The operation of this rule is illustrated in the case of *In Re Haughey*,[38] where the provisions of s 3(4) of the Committee of Public Accounts of Dáil Éireann (Privilege and Procedure) Act 1970 was examined for its constitutionality on questions of contempt. The specific section stated that any witness that refused to answer questions that the committee might "certify the offence of that person under the hand of the chairman of the committee to the High Court" and that the High Court might "after such inquiry as it thinks proper to make, punish or take steps for the punishment of that person in like manner as if he had been guilty of contempt of the High Court.[39] There were two possible interpretations for this section. First, that the committee was imbuing itself with the powers of the High Court to find the non-co-operating witness guilty of contempt. Secondly, that the committee could refer the matter for adjudication by the High Court. The first interpretation would render the section unconstitutional as only the courts established by the Constitution have the power to determine this issue.[40] The second interpretation was that the committee could send the accused to the High Court for it to consider the conduct of the accused in line with the section. As the second interpretation was constitutional, this was preferred by the courts.

## 8.3 Judicial Review and the Constitution

The process of judicial review allows for citizens to litigate their rights against the State under the Constitution. Normally this process involves a citizen claiming that legislation affecting them is contrary to the Constitution. Any application seeking a declaration of unconstitutionality must first rebut the presumption of constitutionality.[41] The effect of a declaration of unconstitutionality

---

[38] [1972] 1 IR 217.
[39] *ibid* at 217.
[40] Art 34.3.1°.
[41] See section 8.2 on the rules of interpretation, and in particular, the presumption of Constitutionality in section 8.2.6.

is that the offending section is unconstitutional and ceases to have legal effect. Where the entirety of the legislation is deemed to be unconstitutional, then the entire Act no longer has any legal effect. This is separate to the declaration of incompatibility under the European Convention on Human Rights Act 2003, where under s 5 of the Act, the most punitive sanction is that the government is advised of the incompatibility of the legislation but the offending legislation still continues to have legal force.

The application for unconstitutionality must commence in the High Court. It may then move on to the Court of Appeal, and then the Supreme Court. Previously there was a provision in Art 34.4.5° which prevented dissenting judgments from being issued on the question of the constitutionality of legislation. However, this was removed and replaced when the 33rd Amendment to the Constitution to establish the Court of Appeal was passed.

The main provisions for the judicial review of legislation are contained in Art 34. The first bar to any application to seek unconstitutionality of legislation is where the legislation in question has already been the subject of an Art 26 reference. The Art 26 reference allows for the President to send a Bill to the Supreme Court to test its constitutionality.[42] Where this process has resulted in a Bill being found to be constitutional, the President must sign the Bill into law but it also bars any individual from seeking judicial review of the same legislation at any point in the future.

Any individual seeking judicial review of legislation must have locus standi, in that they are personally affected by the effect of the legislation in question. However, the test is not applied as strictly as in other cases. For example, in *Society for the Protection of the Unborn Child v Coogan*,[43] interest groups were allowed to plead a breach of the Constitution with regard to the dissemination of abortion services information. In *Crotty v An Taoiseach*,[44] the Supreme Court allowed for a challenge to be taken to the government's attempt to ratify the Single European Act without reference to the people. In this case, even though the applicant would not be personally affected, their application was on the basis of the rights and interests of the general citizens. However, as with all judicial review applications, leave will not be granted where the court is of the opinion that the application is vexatious, frivolous or could be viewed as an abuse of process.

---

[42] See further section 4.1 on the powers of the President.
[43] [1989] IR 734.
[44] [1987] IR 713.

Even though the courts do not have the power to compel the State to spend central funds to protect the rights of citizens through the Constitution, the court will still tend to hear the application. It must be noted that judicial review is an entirely discretionary remedy and the applicant will require an arguable case and stateable grounds for relief. He must also demonstrate that judicial review is an effective remedy in the case at hand. The court may refuse leave if it there is a lack of good faith, delay, lack of evidence or where no useful and legitimate purpose would be served.

All issues grounding the application to seek judicial review must be in a grounding affidavit. Variations may be allowed when the application is heard and the other side must be given a copy of any alterations. As judicial review is viewed as a quick remedy, there are tight time limits as set out in the Rules of the Superior Courts. If leave is denied, then it is possible to appeal this decision to the Supreme Court. The procedure is set out in Ord 58, r 13 of the Rules of the Superior Court.

## 8.4 Constitutional Law Reform

Apart from the mechanisms to reform the Constitution by means of referendum and interpretation, over the lifetime of the Constitution, a number of bodies have been convened to review the document in light of social and societal changes that have transpired over the duration of the Constitution.

The major catalysts for constitution reform have been the legal and political impacts of Northern Ireland on the Constitution, Ireland's membership and continuing obligations under the European Union, socio-economic and societal change in Ireland, international human rights obligations and the working experience of the Constitution over many years.

The first review of the constitution was instigated by Taoiseach Séan Lemass who convened an informal Oireachtas Committee to review the Constitution in 1966. This resulted in a draft report being issued by a legal committee chaired by the Attorney General.

The 1972 Inter-Party Committee on Irish unity addressed issues related to Northern Ireland. This work continued under the auspices of the 1973 All-Party Oireachtas Committee on Irish Relations. Again this committee's work was supplemented by the 1982 Constitution Review body which was comprised of a group of legal experts under the chair of the Attorney General. None of these committees published a report on their findings.

In 1983, the New Ireland Forum was established to review the constitutional provisions relating to Ireland and was comprised of members of Fianna Fáil, Fine Gael, Labour and the SDLP to reflect the views of people from Northern Ireland in their deliberations. This body reported in 1984[45] and made some recommendations on general measures that could restore peace to Northern Ireland that had constitutional ramifications, particularly on the old framework of Arts 2 and 3.[46] These issues were also addressed in the Forum for Peace and Reconciliation which was established by the government in 1994.

### 8.4.1 Constitution Review Group and All-Party Oireachtas Committee on the Constitution

The first major attempt at assessing the need for reform of the Constitution was the Constitution Review Group which was chaired by Dr TK Whitaker. This document[47] worked through each Article of the Constitution, including the Preamble, to assess its purpose, relevancy and proposals for reform in a detailed manner. The review group then reached a conclusion on the future direction and proposals for reform of each article. The conclusion reached by this review group was that the "constitution is a fundamentally sound document that commands the respect of the people and serves them well."[48] But the review did suggest that some amendments are "necessary or desirable in order to renew the Constitution fully'.[49] The work of the Constitution Review Group then led to the establishment of the All-Party Oireachtas Committee on the Constitution which has periodically reported on various aspects of constitutional reform.

The All-Party Oireachtas Committee has reviewed the reform of the Constitution on a thematic basis. It has, to date, published ten reports,[50] but its work has now been superseded by both the Constitutional Convention and the Citizens' Assembly. The First Progress Report published in 1997 dealt with the amendment of the Constitution by referendum, constitutional renewal including an omnibus proposal of technical and minor amendments and gender neutral language, the constitutionality of legislation, local government, electoral and

---

45  *New Ireland Forum Report* (2 May 1984), available at http://cain.ulst.ac.uk/issues/politics/nifr.htm (accessed 10 February 2018).
46  See in particular chapter 3 dealing with the Nation and State.
47  *Report of the Constitution Review Group* (July 1996), available at http://archive.constitution.ie/reports/crg.pdf (accessed 9 February 2018).
48  See http://archive.constitution.ie/constitutional-reviews/default.asp?UserLang=EN (accessed 9 February 2018).
49  See http://archive.constitution.ie/constitutional-reviews/default.asp?UserLang=EN (accessed 9 February 2018).
50  Available at http://archive.constitution.ie/publications/default.asp?UserLang=EN.

ethics commissions, the Ombudsman and the position of women in the home. The Second Report dealt with the position of the Seanad and was published in 1997. The Third Report published in 1998 dealt with the Office of President. The Fourth Report looked at the courts and the judiciary and was published in 1999. In 2000, the Fifth Report looked at the issue of abortion and the Irish Constitution. The Sixth Report examined the referendum process and was published in 2001. The Seventh Report looked at the parliament and its Constitutional foundations. This was published in 2002. The Eighth Report examined the constitutional framework surrounding the operation of government and was published in 2003. The Ninth Report was published in 2004 and concerned the constitutional provisions relating to private property. The final report to date was published in 2006 concerning the family. In addition to these reports the All-Party Oireachtas Committee commissioned two separate reports on a "New Electoral System for Ireland?" by Michael Laver and a study of the Irish Text of the Constitution by Micheál Ó Cearúil, with original contributions by Professor Máirtín Ó Murchú. All these reports are available on the website of the Constitutional Convention.

### 8.4.2 Constitutional Convention

The Constitutional Convention was established by a Resolution of the Houses of the Oireachtas in July 2012 and was tasked with considering a number of constitutional issues, namely: reduction of the Presidential term of office to five years and the alignment with local and European elections, reduction of the voting age to 17, review of the Dáil electoral system, Irish citizens' right to vote at Irish embassies in Presidential elections, provisions for same-sex marriage, amendment of the clause on the role of women in the home and encouraging greater participation of women in public life, Increasing the participation of women in politics; and the removal of the offence of blasphemy from the Constitution. The political background to the Conventions establishment came from the election manifestos of both Labour and Fine Gael that both sought varying degrees of constitutional change as part of their general election policy platforms. Both Fine Gael and Labour made up the coalition government and agreed on the establishment of the Convention as part of their programme for government.

The Convention was adapted from a political science experiment known as 'We the Citizens'. Its aim was to introduce deliberative democracy and group decision-making to Ireland after successful attempts in other European Countries.[51] The Convention was made up

---

[51]  DM Farrell, E O'Malley and J Suiter, "Deliberative Democracy in Action Irish-

primarily of 66 ordinary citizens with the balance being made up of politicians from both North and South of the Border. The Convention received opinions from both invited experts and those involved in the requisite areas and votes on the proposals that are agreed by consensus amongst the group. All submissions made are open to public access on the Commission's website and the majority of the meetings have been live streamed.

The result of the recommendations of the Convention were reported on to government after each topic was voted on. The First Report of the Convention looked at reducing the voting age to 17 and reducing the Presidential term of office to five years and aligning the vote with the local and European elections. The Convention recommended that the voting age be brought to 16 and did not recommend altering the electoral cycle for the office of president.

The Second Report looked at amending the clause on the role of women and encouraging the greater participation of women in public life. It also considered how to increase the participation of women in public life. There were two constitutional amendments recommended. The first was to amend the provisions of Art 41.2.1° to make the provisions gender neutral and recognise the work of carers. In particular, the Report conveyed the wishes of the Convention that the State, through amendment of the Constitution, recognises a "reasonable level of support" to ensure that carers "shall not be obliged by economic necessity to engage in labour".[52] Regarding increasing the participation of women in public life, the Convention recommended an explicit provision on gender equality but did not endorse a particular constitutional provision on enhancing participation in public life, although it recommended government action on this issue.[53]

The Third Report of the Convention was on the issue of marriage equality which overwhelmingly recommended constitutional change in this regard. The report details the manner in which the change is recommended. The recommendation formed part of the successful Marriage Equality Referendum which was the 34th Amendment to the Constitution. However, there was already cross-party support for

---

style: The 2011 We the Citizens Pilot Citizens' Assembly" (2013) 28 (1) *Irish Political Studies* 99.

[52] *Second Report of the Convention on the Constitution* (May 2013), available at https://www.constitution.ie/AttachmentDownload.ashx?mid=268d9308-c9b7-e211-a5a0-005056a32ee4 (accessed 9 February 2018).

[53] Some governmental action has been seen on this point with the introduction of gender quotas for political parties through the Electoral (Political Funding) Act 2014.

the referendum in the Oireachtas before this issue was set before the Constitutional Convention.

The Fourth Report of the Convention dealt with proposals to amend the Dáil electoral system. The ballot was in favour of retaining the current electoral system.[54] The Convention also recommended the establishment of an Electoral Commission and other ancillary issues. The Fifth Report of the Convention recommended the Irish citizens' right to vote at Irish embassies in presidential elections and there is a referendum proposed by the government on this issue. The Sixth Report was on the issue of blasphemy. The Convention recommended the removal of blasphemy from the Constitution and its replacement with a general provision to include incitement to religious hatred. A referendum has been proposed to give effect to these recommendations.

The Convention members also selected a number of their own themes that they considered important to constitutional reform. The first issue was Dáil reform and comprised the Seventh Report of the Convention. The members recommended a number of changes, some of which would require referendums. The Convention members recommended a constitutional position for the Ceann Comhairle and Dáil committees. They also recommended an amendment to Art 17.2 regarding expenditure proposals. Regarding the Ceann Comhairle, the convention recommended that election to the position would be carried out by secret ballot, and this has already been changed in the rules governing Dáil Business by means of changes to the standing orders.

The Eighth Report of the Convention addressed the constitutional recognition of economic, social and cultural rights. The Convention recommended changes to the Constitution to reflect these rights, but did accede that these issues should be referred elsewhere to consider the implications of these reforms. However, the Convention made explicit reference to the incorporation of housing, social security, rights for those with disabilities, healthcare and language and cultural rights as part of a process of constitutional reform.

### 8.4.3 Citizens' Assembly

The Citizens' Assembly was built from the framework of the previous Constitutional Convention in that the mechanics of deliberation and decision making were mirrored from the Convention. The Assembly was constituted after the Convention had finished its programme of

---

[54] See the electoral system in the organs of government as discussed in section 5.2.7.

work. The Assembly's remit goes beyond purely constitutional change to dealing with broader societal change facing Ireland. However, its first topic for deliberation was the right to life under the Irish Constitution. The Assembly will also look at the constitutional considerations on the issue of fixed term parliaments and the mechanics of referendums. Outside of the parameters of the constitution, the Assembly will also look at tackling climate change and responding to an aging population. The Assembly was established by a resolution of Seanad Éireann on Friday 15 July 2016.[55]

The Assembly is chaired by Ms Justice Mary Laffoy and had its first meeting in October 2016. The Assembly is made up of 100 people comprising of the Chair and 99 citizens eligible to vote at referendums and was randomly selected to comprise of a broad sample of Irish society.

The Assembly is to make a report comprising of recommendations to a committee of both Houses of the Oireachtas. As with the Constitutional Convention, an expert advisory group has been established to aid in the Assembly's work. Submissions may be made on any of the topics of deliberation by members of the public and the Assembly may also invite submissions from interested bodies and seek expert advice on particular issues. Issues are determined by a majority vote of the members. The Chair has a casting vote. The government is to provide responses to the recommendations made by the Assembly in the Houses of the Oireachtas, and if they accept the recommendation they will indicate the timeframe envisaged for the holding of related referendums.

---

[55]  246(16) *Seanad Éireann Debate* 1.

# INDEX